MASTERING EMAIL

MARKETING:

A Complete Guide to Boosting Your

Business with Winning Strategies.

Sam Austin

TABLE OF CONTENTS

Chapter 1
Chapter 2
Chapter 3
Chapter 4
Chapter 5
Chapter 6
Chapter 7
Chapter 8
Chapter 9
Chapter 10
Chapter 11
Chapter 12
Chapter 13
Chapter 14
Chapter 15
Chapter 16
Chapter 17
Chapter 18
Chapter 19

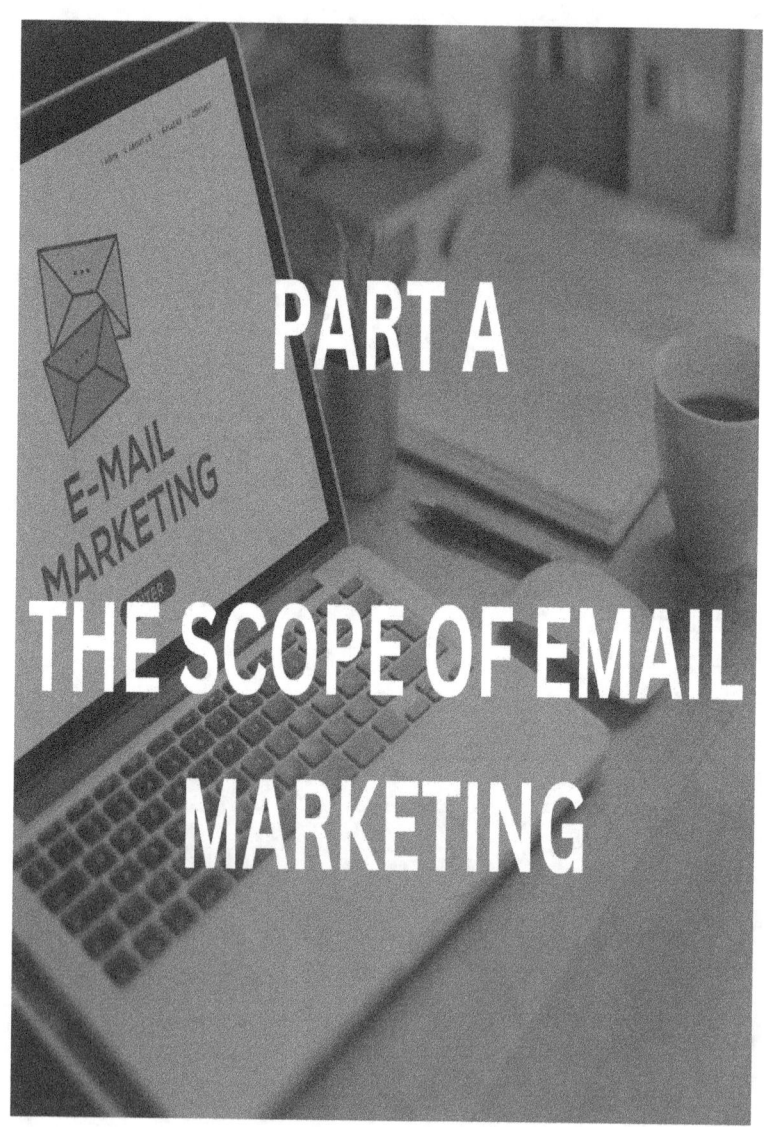

PART A

THE SCOPE OF EMAIL

MARKETING

Chapter 1

The Meaning, Types, Pros, and Cons of Email Marketing

The practice of marketing or promoting products or services by sending a promotional message via email is known as email marketing. Any email sent to a client, past or present, could be considered email marketing, depending on how it is defined broadly. It entails making requests for contracts, donations, or purchases, as well as sending promotional emails.

Building loyalty, trust, and brand awareness are the three main goals that email marketing strategies typically aim to accomplish. The term typically refers to sending emails with the goal of enhancing a company's relationship with current or former customers, encouraging customer loyalty and repeat business, luring in new clients, persuading existing clients to make an immediate purchase, and disseminating third-party advertisements.

Terms used in Email Marketing

The following are some terms used in email marketing:

1. Email Campaign: This involves talking to people about your products or services to convince them to buy or use them. It is also referred to as an "email blast."

2. Solo Advertisements: Except for the fact that the subscribers are not your

own but rather someone else's, this is comparable to an email campaign.

3. Analytics: This exhibits the outcomes of campaign solo ads. Examples of results include the open rate, click-through rate, return click-through rate, location, time, and the number of people who engaged in conversation.

4. Newsletter: This is a recurring message that is sent to your subscribers regularly to either update them on previous messages or remind them of new ones.

5. Conversion: This is when the campaign's objective is achieved.

6. Workflow: This is a notification that customers receive after an action is completed on a website.

Types of Email Marketing Campaigns

The four most common types of email marketing campaigns are listed below, along with some tips on how to use each of them to expand your company.

1. Email Newsletter

The newsletter is one of the most widespread and widely used email marketing strategies. An email newsletter is a great tool for small businesses to share useful information and resources with their subscribers. It's crucial to add value to your subscribers' inboxes; to do this, make interesting content and include thought leadership, tutorials, and announcements about brand-new products or services. Asking whether the content fosters relationships with subscribers, boosts retention and engagement, and increases subscribers' loyalty will help you determine how effective your newsletter is.

2. Acquisition Emails

This can aid in bringing in customers who have chosen to receive your emails but haven't yet become paying clients. You can convince those on your email list of the benefits of becoming frequent customers by producing alluring offers and educational content. Acquisition emails are a fantastic way to target users who have shown some interest in your company's products or services, grow your business and generate more revenue, and move leads through the conversion funnel more quickly.

3. Retention Emails

If you've used email marketing campaigns in the past, think about using retention emails for your small business. Your small business can maintain contact with subscribers by sending them a message asking for feedback or making an offer if they haven't recently interacted with your company or email campaigns. Utilizing retention emails is a highly effective campaign strategy that can help you keep the customers you've worked so hard to win.

4. Promotional Emails

To increase sales, signups, and new product offerings for your small business, consider using promotional emails. Promotional emails contain discounts and other incentives that persuade and exhort your target audience to purchase a new good or service. Use promotional emails to inform subscribers about new products or services, offer exclusive discounts to devoted clients, and upsell more items.

One effective strategy for attracting, keeping, and engaging customers is email marketing. Your small business can profit significantly by implementing an effective email marketing campaign. To accomplish your small business objectives, make sure to choose the appropriate email marketing campaign. Remember that when your customer or target finds your email to be extremely valuable, they are more likely to forward it and/or share it with others (always include your social media share buttons in your emails).

The Pros of Email Marketing

1. It's an inexpensive strategy for attracting your target audience's attention.

To reach and engage customers, email marketing is a very economical strategy. Your cost for running an effective email campaign can be very low if you can write your emails and develop an internal email strategy. You can manage thousands of considerate and efficient emails each month even with the low investment of a basic client management software system.

2. It facilitates the development of strong relationships with clients.

Sending customers an email is a fantastic way to connect with them personally and specifically. Customers will learn more about your business, develop a sense of trust, and make more purchases if you create emails that accurately reflect your brand.

3. It promotes and increases awareness of brands.

The brand of your business extends far beyond your company's logo. Your reputation in the market is based on your brand. Your emails' tone, look, and the content will all contribute to building your distinctive brand.

4. It can be quickly and easily created and launched.

A marketing email can be written and sent in a matter of minutes as opposed to more traditional marketing campaigns, which require more time for design, production, and distribution.

5. It is highly modifiable.

Email can be modified to support a more specialized customer experience with a few simple keystrokes. If you take the time to fully understand your target audience, email can be a powerful engagement tool.

6. The collection and monitoring of data and analytics are simple.

The value of data in business is increasing, and it aids in customer understanding. With the help of email, you can record and keep track of a wealth of data, enabling you to determine who opens, reads, and responds to each email.

7. It can draw visitors to your website.

Customers can be attracted to your website with the aid of an email campaign that has interesting content and a clear call-to-action (CTA).

8. It is simple to share.

The "forward" key on the keyboard is conveniently located for customers to send information to a friend. Make sure the subject line of your emails can be read by a variety of recipients. About 76% of Americans (or 248.7 million) use email, and many of them check it frequently (typically on their mobile device). Three out of four people use email.

The Cons of Email Marketing

1. The majority of people won't open your email.

Your emails may very well get lost in the flood of emails that most people receive due to their high volume. You can stand out in a crowded inbox by writing personalized, interesting emails.

2. Consistency and regular updating are needed.

Emails and email campaigns need to be well-maintained and frequently updated. Customers will continue to want more if new content and information are consistently available.

3. The race against time is like a sea around you.

How can you tell if your email is even being read when so many people and companies use the internet? To make each email campaign better, use data to track click-through, read-rate, and traffic.

4. Your emails' effectiveness depends on their design, tone, and strategy.

When using email marketing, think carefully about your strategy. When emails are put together in a hurry, they may emphasize the wrong brands.

5. Emails sometimes come off as impersonal.

Even though emails can be personalized, they cannot replace the value of interpersonal communication. Even in digital communication, keep your attention on actual people.

6. It's simple to find the unsubscribe button.

Your leads and customers can unsubscribe from your emails just as easily as you can. Customers can easily unsubscribe and disappear if they become dissatisfied with the frequency or content of emails.

Chapter 2

Form Page and Landing Page

Form Page

An opt-in box known as a "form page" can be embedded on your website or made to appear automatically when a page is viewed. This is a single-page website that collects data on your subscribers. It's also referred to as an opt-in form, a signup form, or a capture page. It enables the entry of data by the user, which is then processed by a server. Because web users fill out the forms using checkboxes, buttons, or text fields, they sometimes resemble paper forms or database forms. For instance, forms can be used to enter shipping or payment information when placing an online order for a product or to access search engine results.

Importance of Form page

1. Clients prefer options

Some people find it time-consuming to call a company's phone number, while others would rather speak with a representative directly. By giving your customers a choice of all available contact options (including a phone number, email address, physical address, and web form), you allow them to use the one they prefer and avoid customer annoyance when their preferred method isn't available.

2. Get the information you require

Web forms are unique because they give you the flexibility to decide what kinds of information you want to collect from your customers. By specifying the fields you need and making clear which of those fields are required, you can make sure that visitors to your website are giving you the information you need. Simple email addresses encourage communication that is unstructured and undirected. Various tactical newsletters or sections of your website collect various information for various recipients. Each designated form page is managed by the CRM, and all data is collected automatically.

3. Forms can be tracked

Professional form page management not only enables you to make changes that instantly update the website or newsletter, but the reporting systems also provide priceless data regarding the client's navigation before completing the form.

4. Supporting inquiries

The CRM and newsletter automatically update a client's information using all the data fields.

5. The most important factor is convenience

Using professional form pages and clickable email links that open your customers' default email client prevents all potential issues.

6. Connect to external applications like Zapier, Capsule CRM or Salesforce, MailChimp, or Stripe for online payments in a matter of seconds.

Landing Page

This website is a microsite. It is the first page you see after clicking on an advertisement or an email campaign. A landing page is an excellent tool for boosting SEO, growing your audience, and building your brand. Furthermore, it could be included in a successful PPC strategy. Landing pages are used by about 68% of B2B businesses to generate leads that can then be converted. Fortunately, 44% of these clicks go to home pages.

Customers are encouraged to take action by being directed to specific products, services, or offers on landing pages. It is possible to generate conversions and build a customer base. The terms opt-in pages, sales pages, product pages, static pages, squeeze pages, single property pages, static pages, and squeeze pages are also used to describe landing pages.

Importance of Landing Page

1. They focus on the offer rather than the business.

Your potential customers are clicking for a reason, so it's not a good idea to mislead them by failing to deliver on your promise. It is not appropriate at this time to provide a detailed history of your business. This is not to say that the brand of your business shouldn't be linked to the landing page. Quite the opposite, they should serve a separate function while complementing your brand.

2. They are undistracted and concentrating.

The content on your landing page should be written to obtain the user's desired outcome while they complete the registration process.

3. The forms are not difficult to fill out.

Long forms can intimidate visitors and tempt them to leave rather than take advantage of the chance you are offering. If you can't make your form any shorter, break it down into steps so the user can see where they are in the process.

4. They address a specific group of people.

By dividing up your customer base, you can use niche marketing strategies to target specific consumers. If you have a base that responds well to a particular offer, like an eBook or discount, your landing page can function as a built-in segmentation tool, allowing you to nurture these leads effectively moving forward.

5. They gather specific data about your potential customers.

Speaking of targeted audiences, even if you attract the right crowd, you won't be able to convert them if you don't gather the appropriate data. More than just a name and email address should be included in the collection of demographic data. Additionally, it should help you understand why a person clicked and what their potential long-term relationship with your business is.

6. They offer a place for your promotional offers.

Your online special offers will not help your business grow if they are not linked to landing pages. By creating landing pages, you give your offers a place to live.

7. They express gratitude.

There should always be a thank-you page after your landing page. This not only shows good manners but also reassures the customer that the registration process has been completed.

8. They give users access to additional marketing channels.

You just made an offer, and a customer likes it. You can now offer clickable links to other offers, your social media accounts, or a subscription form for an email list. There is no denying that we live in a connected digital world. One of the best investments you can make for your company is to move forward with a digital marketing campaign. The inclusion of landing pages as you develop your digital marketing toolkit is a wise choice that will benefit both you and your customers.

Types of Landing Pages

1. Standalone landing pages

These consist of infomercials, viral landing pages, click-through, and lead capture (also known as lead generation or squeeze pages).

a. Click-Through Landing Pages

This kind of landing page is extremely simple. The only objective is to provide a prospect with all the details they need about an offer, outlining the benefits and the context of use in a way that will convince them to proceed to the point of purchase. Simply be sincere about the offer and visit the company's website, where they will convince you to complete the transaction.

b. Lead Capture Landing Pages

The purpose of lead capture landing pages, also referred to as squeeze pages, is to gather visitors' personal data, usually beginning with their name and email address. One button for entering your information is all that is present on a true squeeze page; there are no navigational links or other buttons. Usually, a reward is given in exchange for this private information. Building an email list of relevant potential customers is the reason a business would use a lead capture landing page. These people will then be targeted with future marketing using this list.

c. Infomercial Landing Pages

The infomercials of online marketing are these landing pages. They function by using the same boisterous language that you've seen on those fake WOW TV commercials, and they're typically about 50 feet long (a lot of scrolling). As they read further down the page, the reader becomes more engaged with the sales message and is more determined to keep reading because it took some effort for them to get there.

d. Viral Landing Pages

Businesses that attempt to generate viral buzz typically do so to increase their visibility. Examples of this kind of page frequently include entertaining flash games or humorous videos. Whether it's a small logo, a "powered by" mention in the video, or oblique product references in the game or video, they'll make a subtle reference to the business that made the work.

2. Microsites

Microsites are extra-small websites that are used in conjunction with larger campaigns. They typically have a vanity URL associated with the timing and relevance of the campaign. Despite the volume of pages, It continues to be categorized as a landing page because customers are directed there from paid online advertisements as well as print and television advertisements.

This format is frequently used by automakers, who create specialized microsites for each type of vehicle they make. They often have higher-quality, more expensive designs and are frequently created in Flash. When localized dealerships receive the microsite as part of a co-branding arrangement, it enables them to deliver more consistent sales messaging for their marketing initiatives.

Movie trailer websites are another popular application of microsites. They don't require the infrastructure of a permanent website because they are popular sites that only exist to promote the movie.

3. Product Detail Landing Pages

The product detail landing page is a popular design for landing pages in the retail sector.

The information about the offered product is only available on this page of the main website. The advantage of this kind of landing page is that it doesn't involve any additional work to create a different page.

However, since it's a component of the entire website, it comes with a full complement of distractions, such as navigation, links, banners, and more, all of which can divert customers from taking the desired action, making it more difficult to measure the effectiveness of your campaigns. If your success metric is the purchase of the original landing page item, they might stray off and buy something else, which is fine, but it sends conflicting signals for tracking purposes because they might appear as non-converting customers.

The use of the home page as a Landing Page

This is the least efficient type of landing page, and as a result, it converts at the lowest rate. Too frequently, marketers will invest a lot of money into campaigns that only direct people to the home page.

Why does this matter? as a result of the excessive distractions. A successful landing page must have a single, clear goal as its fundamental tenet. With the help of a targeted landing page, you can assess the success of your campaign from beginning to end and make adjustments to the messaging, offer, and ad copy until you achieve the best results. How? The banners and Google Adwords ads aren't doing their jobs if nobody visits your landing pages. Your landing page is not optimized if visitors arrive there but do not convert.

In summary, it's predicted that using a standalone landing page instead of directing visitors to your homepage will boost conversion rates by about 25%. Simple A/B testing can boost conversion rates on your landing page by a factor of 2 to 10.

How to make a landing page with a high conversion rate

While there are many tools available for creating landing pages and each one is different, the most effective ones frequently share the following five characteristics:

1. An attractive offer

Two things should be immediately clear to visitors when they land on your landing page:

    a. what you're offering

    b. why they will benefit from whatever it is you're offering.

You need to communicate these two points succinctly and as soon as the page loads to make clicking your CTA seems like a simple choice.

2. Captivating images or videos

The effectiveness of a landing page can be significantly impacted by its visuals. Every visitor has a chance to be positively impacted by your use of images and videos. Each image you use should clearly state its purpose and, ideally, show your product in the appropriate environment.

As with every element on a landing page, the purpose of your visuals is to persuade the visitor to click your CTA. Using creativity that evokes a feeling in the viewer is among the best ways to achieve this anticipation, apprehension about missing out, inspiration, optimism, etc.

Visitors who are not captivated by your visuals will not be motivated to act. The objective should be to demonstrate to visitors how your product or service can improve their lives using images or videos.

3. Additional writing

The most important thing to do in this situation is to provide more information about your offer.

a. Who benefits from this?

b. What distinguishing qualities best describe your offering?

c. Why can't someone afford to pass up on this opportunity?

Consider the visitor and their interests as you write the supporting copy. This copy should support your offer and guide the visitor toward conversion.

4. A direct call to action

The purpose of every landing page is to persuade the visitor to click the call to action (CTA). A CTA typically consists of a button that encourages website visitors to take a specific action. Examples include "Get Started," "Sign Up," and "Buy Now."

There are many CTAs you can use, but these suggestions will help you create one that is very clickable.

    a. Choosing a contrasting color will help your CTA button stand out from the rest of the page's content. Use a color that stands out against the background and grabs the viewer's attention.

Features of background colors on landing pages and CTA

Colors	Features
Yellow	Inspiring, Youthful, and Captivating
Red	Vitality, urgency (often used in clearance sales)
Orange	Violent (excellent for CTA buttons)
Pink	Lovely, feminine (great for women only)
Blue	Trust, Security (Banks, Accountants)
Green	Wealth, finance, and entertainment (eye-friendly colors)
Purple	Calming, soothing (beauty and anti-aging products)

Black	Strong, (Luxurious Sophisticated)	Sleek &

b. Make the action clear: Users should be able to tell what will happen when they click the button. For instance, clicking "Buy now" will start a purchase, and clicking "Take the quiz" above will start a quiz to help you choose the best pair of eyeglasses. The generic nature of CTA copy like "Next" or "Click here" will leave visitors unsure of what action to take.

5. Social Evidence

Your best conversion technique is this. For instance, if there is a line outside a café, that indicates that the café must be good. Similarly, if a trustworthy friend tells you about a new brand, that is typically all you need to know to believe that brand.

One of the best methods for convincing visitors to your landing page to act is to use social evidence. Consider how you could include:

a. Customer feedback
b. Successful case studies
c. Social media recommendations
d. Recognizable customer logos or avatars of famous users of your product or service
e. Reviews from reputable sites like TripAdvisor, Yelp, and Trustpilot

f. Press mentions in well-known publications

Important components that must be present on a landing page

a. Awesome Headline: It must be concise, uncomplicated, goal-oriented, and have a compelling subheadline.

b. Amazing Image: No Stock Images.

c. Justification: Why do you act the way that you do? What distinguishes you from others?

d. The benefit with clear value: What will I gain? How will my life improve as a result?

e. Logical Flow: Explanation > Benefits > Testimonies > CTA

f. Identify the pain: What is the pain? What is the issue?

g. Something about Pleasure: What if you could..., How would your life change if... etc

h. Verified Testimonial: relevant to the product or service, including name, city, and picture.

i. A Guarantee: Return of funds, outcomes, and timeline

j. Impressive CTA: Powerful words with Colorful CTA buttons

k. Trust-related metrics: Customer logos, affiliations, and certifications

l. Videos: Associated with Product or Service, Avoid Selling and Instead, Provide Assistance

m. A/B Testing: Google Optimization

n. Get rid of navigational ability: Streamline Navigation

Best Practices for Landing Pages

A landing page attracts the customer's attention, creating a positive first impression, and typically includes several landing page best practices developed over time. Best practices for desktop and mobile have some differences, but in general, landing pages with particular components have higher conversion rates.

The following are examples of best practices for landing pages:

1. **Make sure the call to action, headlines, and main message are all visible above the fold.**

In the past, newspapers used a concept called "above the fold," in which the most significant headlines and news were printed on the top half of the first page. In terms of digital marketing, this is the portion of the screen that is visible to the user without having to scroll down. When a user first arrives at the landing page, there's a good chance they'll scan the entire page without scrolling down to read more. To increase the chance of receiving a response, keep the headlines, the main message, and the call-to-action (CTA) above the fold. The headline must be precise, short, and contain the primary keyword to be effective for SEO.

1. Utilize just one call to action (CTA)

Every landing page must be customized to fulfill a single goal. It might involve a limited-time offer, a risk-free trial, a contest entry, signing up for a webinar, or downloading an eBook. You should only have one CTA button above the fold because too many CTAs or links to other pages will divert the viewer from the main objective.

2. The call to action (CTA) should be repeated as necessary.

It should not be necessary for a desktop or mobile user to scroll up after reading the landing page copy to see the CTA. An exact copy of the CTA should be placed in the lower portion of the page to keep the potential customer's attention.

3. Design of the CTA button

The call to action (CTA) button must visually entice the viewer to click it. It ought to be the right size and contrast with the background color of the landing page. A CTA that is repeated on the landing page must be an exact duplicate of the CTA that is displayed above the fold.

4. Mobile-friendly design

Designing landing pages for mobile use is crucial because data shows that 56.89% of all internet traffic worldwide occurs on a mobile device. Since many B2B businesses use computers to conduct business, there are still plenty of reasons to design for older users' desktop computers. Your audience's preferred devices should be determined by your analytics data.

5. Optimization of the traffic sources

Create the landing page according to the traffic sources you use. Short, copy-focused landing pages convert more effectively than pages optimized for SEO. Keep landing pages for sources of paid traffic brief, direct, and clear messages and calls to action.

6. Present a social proof

A persuasive strategy that works well is the fear of missing out. To increase the conversion rate of your landing pages, use user testimonials and reviews. Users are more likely to trust and believe in your brand when they discover that other clients and companies find value in it.

The differences between Form Page and Landing Page

Form Page	Landing Page
It is an opt-in that is directly integrated into your blog or website.	It's a standalone opt-in that can be utilized with or without a website.

It must serve many purposes; for instance, a typical homepage typically has some form of navigation bar near the top.	A landing page's only goal is to convert traffic (viewers). Landing pages with a focus on simplicity and effectiveness Actually, there are only three possibilities: Convert, Login, and Exit the Page.
It must contain a variety of contents.	A landing should only contain content that is relevant to the offer, good, or service that you're trying to promote.

Because it is primarily used as a resource, it lacks a strong and noticeable CTA.	The landing page encourages users to take action.

Chapter 3

Email Campaign

An email campaign is a series of marketing initiatives that reach out to many recipients at once. Email campaigns are designed to send relevant offers and helpful content to subscribers at the most efficient times. By using email campaigns, you can build solid, trustworthy relationships with your customers.

The subject of the email, the audience's lifestyle and habits, and the day of the week all play a role in determining when to send an email campaign. Given that Monday is the busiest day of the week and Friday is the least busy, the best days are typically Tuesday, Wednesday, and Thursday. People make an effort to complete the tasks for the current week without leaving anything for the following week. Because Saturday and Sunday are frequently family days, most people spend their weekends relaxing and avoiding email.

The most ideal times are:

➢ At 6 a.m., a lot of people have the habit of checking their phones in bed.

➢ Because people begin their workdays by checking their emails at around 10 a.m.

➢ Because of lunch or coffee breaks, around 2 pm.

➤ From 8 p.m. to midnight, because this is when most people are free and many of them read emails before going to bed.

However, in most situations, it's much simpler to determine when to send email campaigns because it's inconvenient for people to read emails during rush hour when they're traveling to and from work and at night. All in all, there's a chance of waking them up. You should stay away from these hours.

A/B testing is necessary to determine when to send emails based on your industry. The effectiveness of the email campaign is evaluated by A/B tests using open and click-through rates.

Once you know when your business should send email campaigns, you can efficiently schedule them using the following email service provider types: one-time email campaigns or newsletters, autoresponders, and email marketing automation.

Chapter 4

Newsletter

This is an ongoing message that you send to your subscribers, either to update them on previous messages or to remind them of new information.

Important Components of a Great Newsletter

1. Brevity

Another lengthy newsletter won't do anyone any good because we are already overloaded with information. Try to keep your document to one page rather than trying to fit everything into it. Shorter, more frequent deliveries are preferred to infrequent ones.

2. Storytelling

The best newsletters make use of traditional story-telling methods. To engage your reader, adopt a conversational style. Share a few insider details about your industry. Keep in mind that you're writing a letter, not just reporting the news.

3. Reader attention

Avoid keeping a diary. Your intended audience will be more interested in how you can help them than in hearing about all of your successes and failures. Strong content draws readers to e-newsletters.

4. Call to Action

Let's be straightforward in this situation. None of us would take the time away from our hectic schedules to make a newsletter if we didn't anticipate receiving anything in return. Every newsletter needs to have a clear call to action. This might appear as a coupon, an invitation to an event, or even a request for someone to "like" your Facebook page. Make sure you're asking your audience to take action.

5. Design

Even though many email services offer design templates, you can hire a professional designer to create your newsletter for a reasonable price. An appealing newsletter, whether it be printed or sent via email, will promote readership and help your brand.

One of the best tools you have for reaching out to customers and potential customers is your newsletter. By implementing these strategies, you'll be on the road to success and guarantee that your newsletter is opened and read.

Purpose of a Newsletter

A newsletter's primary functions are to advertise a good or service and establish a personal connection with each of your email subscribers. However, your goals will determine the precise goal of your email newsletter. Outlining specific goals for that campaign is one of the first steps in creating a newsletter.

Objectives might include boosting your open and click-through rates, gaining more subscribers, or producing your best email yet in terms of conversion. Whatever your aim is, try to make sure it's specific and measurable. Given this, you could say that the main goal of email newsletters is to assist your overall email and digital marketing strategy. The goals of each of your newsletters should be consistent with the overall marketing strategy.

Advantages of a Newsletter

Choosing where to spend marketing funds is crucial because advertising and marketing can be among a company's biggest budget expenses. Few marketing tools offer a higher return on investment per dollar than newsletters. Newsletters are an important part of a comprehensive marketing strategy, even though they cannot completely replace other methods of business promotion.

1. Keep Up Relationships

Newsletters are a good, low-effort way to stay in touch with customers or other interested parties. Today's desktop publishing software makes it simple to create newsletters in eye-catching formats and send them instantly to everyone on the business' email list. Regular newsletter distribution serves to remind readers about the business. People are more likely to contact a business they frequently interact with when they need one of the goods or services it provides.

2. Teach and Inform

The sender has complete control over the content, which is a major advantage of newsletters. Newsletters can inform readers about new products, feature employees, celebrate accomplishments, and make announcements about impending occasions or special offers. They can even act as another form of advertising by restricting access to coupons or discounts to subscribers, which is a clever way to monitor readership. The newsletter is a perfect venue for addressing misunderstandings or outlining the company's position if the business has received unfavorable press or customer feedback.

3. Obtain the desired audience

The people who have already shown interest by purchasing a product, applying for a job, or joining the company's email list are the recipients of newsletters, which directly reach the company's target market. The company can address topics that it knows will interest these readers because it is already aware of their purchasing preferences or interests. By informing and keeping the audience up to date without overtly soliciting a sale or contribution, newsletters accomplish this in a friendly, unobtrusive manner.

4. Low Price

Newsletter production is relatively inexpensive in comparison to other forms of advertising and marketing. The majority of newsletters are distributed digitally, so there is no longer any expense for paper or postage. A two- or four-page newsletter can be incorporated into the workloads of current employees without adding a new position. The newsletter gets easier to produce over time once the format and scope have been established, possibly even outlining recurring columns.

Types of Newsletter

1. Pitch newsletter

This particular kind of newsletter highlights the advantages of your goods or services and is distributed to subscribers. It is purported to be employed to persuade your subscribers to make purchases, subscribe to mailing lists, download content, or engage in any other behavior that will aid your company in reaching its sales objectives. A pitch newsletter is typically included in educational materials like emails, brochures, and web pages. Thus, it is also referred to as "sales copy."

The effectiveness of your pitch newsletter may, in some cases, make or break your messaging efforts. Even if your product is outstanding and perfectly satisfies customer needs, if you can't persuade customers of this, they might choose one of your competitors instead.

Customers are pressed for time and constantly confronted with a variety of options that can satisfy their interests and address their issues. They most likely don't have enough time to thoroughly investigate all of their options. That implies that you might only have one opportunity to convince them to join you, and that "one opportunity" is frequently your sales copy.

However, how do you write it? How can you make sure that your written sales pitch persuades potential customers to want to learn more about your company and what it has to offer? Well, there are a few techniques you can employ to position yourself in the best possible way to make sales from your copy.

Guidelines for writing Sales Copy

a. Fix your attention on a single issue.

Sales copy shouldn't generalize everything your company does. It is intended to provoke particular action, not arouse interest. Pick one thing to concentrate on or one area of pain, and stick with it. You might be a copywriter for a company that sells home appliances, for example. You've been given the assignment of creating a sales copy for a brand-new waffle maker the business is releasing. The copy you create must focus on just one problem that the new appliance solves, not a haphazard list of all its features or a general plug for the business.

Choose what you think is the most compelling, marketable benefit or pain point for your product or service and focus on that. You would have a selection to choose from in the waffle iron example. You could talk about how it makes waffles quickly, how it has a new setting that automatically cooks waffles to an even temperature, or how simple it is to clean. Any of those advantages might offer interesting content, but you should only pick one. Otherwise, your sales copy might come off as wordy or disorganized.

b. Be aware of your target audience.

Your sales copy is no exception when it comes to being targeted in all of your messaging. Identify the target market for your product, the reasons why they might like it, and the features or advantages that will appeal to them the most. Making buyer personas for your potential clients is a trustworthy way to identify the target audience for your sales copy.

In the case of the waffle iron, you might discover that the product is appealing to both parents who want to make waffles for their kids and young professionals who are looking for appliances to furnish their kitchens in their first apartments. To fit those molds, you could develop two distinct buyer personas. Although both are potential markets for your product, each would respond better to a different approach to messaging. Therefore, if you were to create a sales copy for the new appliances, you should choose one persona to concentrate on.

c. Make your writing and storytelling interesting.

The primary focus of sales copy is action. In order to convince a customer to take a specific action, usually to make a purchase, you must use persuasive techniques. As corny as it may sound, you cannot convince someone to do something unless you are persuasive enough to do so. That begins with the words you choose to use.

Let's assume for illustration that you have decided to cater your sales copy to the persona of "parents making waffles for their kids." "Are you tired of your old waffle iron?" is not how you want to phrase your copy. Does it not function as it did in the past? Consider upgrading now. Visit the brand-new Waffletron 4000 right now!

That kind of copy is too flimsy, hazy, and bland to excite or engage a potential customer. There's a good chance that a customer would glance over that copy in favor of an alternative that would encourage them to make a purchase. The following would make for a better sales copy: "Kids: the Sunday morning alarm clock you don't get to set." No matter how you feel about it, you have to be awake and on parental duty by 6 a.m. You need to take care of other people's needs before you can spend time with them. All three are facilitated by waffles. See the Waffletron 4000, which is billed as "the best, fastest waffle iron for hitting snooze on Sunday."

The reader is drawn in by the copy and becomes invested in the story. It has a relatable backstory and is focused on problems that the buyer persona would likely encounter in their daily lives.

d. Make sure it is clear, conversational, and easily understood.

Your sales copy shouldn't necessarily be difficult to understand or lengthy. You're not writing a novel or your dissertation; instead, you're creating a succinct soundbite that will persuade someone to purchase a certain item. Write straightforwardly and keep it simple.

Unreadable copies may have the following text:

"Without a doubt, the most innovative and cutting-edge waffle maker available is the Waffletron 4000. You have a plethora of challenging responsibilities as a parent. Without a doubt, every single one of them will be solved by the Waffletron 4000."

The majority of customers won't be interested in that copy because it sounds confusing and pretentious. Never give it too much thought. You want your copy to be compelling, but dramatic doesn't always equate to effective. Consider your copy a pitch. Typically, words like "plethora" and "hence" are not found in pitches. In this instance, simplicity is better.

e. Focus on talking about your product's advantages rather than its features.

It might be tempting to highlight all of the fantastic features of a product you're selling in your copy if it has a lot of bells and whistles. However, you should wait before doing that. You're better off going right to the advantages they'll see because sales copy is supposed to be brief and sweet. Give them an explanation of the outcomes that each of those features will produce.

Sales copy is not a product page; it is a hook. Interest-building and action-instigation are its primary goals. Consumers can then learn about all the fantastic features your product has to offer. Here is an illustration of sales copy that places too much emphasis on the features of the products.

"Consider checking out the Waffletron 4000. It has an outer shell that is temperature-controlled, an automatic golden-brownness monitor, topping holders, and an adjustable waffle timer."
That sales copy is a little too technical and repeats information that the customer should find after being persuaded by the sales copy.

A better copy would read as follows:
"Waffles can cause more trouble than they need to. Finding that golden-brown spot between batter and burn can be challenging. Your waffles will always be perfect—quickly and effortlessly—with the Waffletron 4000."

This copy explains exactly what your customer can expect from the product. It stimulates their curiosity about it. They will independently learn about the specific features once they decide to research the product as a result of the sales copy.

f. Finish with a strong, concise call to action.

There is always a goal in sales copy. It could be written to persuade a customer to make a purchase, sign up for business communications, download a content offer, or engage in any other action that will eventually lead them to your company. Without a strong call to action, none of that will happen. An effective call to action should be easy to spot and provide some context for what will happen when a potential customer clicks on it. Effective calls to action might read as follows:

> ➤ "Download our content offer now."
> ➤ "Book a free consultation today."
> ➤ "Learn more about [A product],"

Giving your prospect a clear course of action is your ultimate objective in this situation. You must provide them with a path to follow if your sales copy persuades them to want to learn more about your company. Calls to action are the beginning of that path.

2. Informative Newsletter

This message is meant to deepen your relationship with your subscribers; you don't intend to promote or try to sell anything to them. One-to-many emails that you can send to your lists to update them on your most recent content, product announcements, and other information are known as informative newsletters.

Note: *Only those who have requested your emails should receive them.*

The following email formats are examples of informative newsletters that you must send to your contacts to keep them informed.

a. New Content Announcement Email

In this email, a single marketing offer is described and promoted, and the call-to-action contains a link to a landing page that is specifically designed for that offer.

The offer itself should be the primary consideration when creating an email for a particular offer. To effectively communicate the value of the offer, the copy should be succinct but descriptive. Additionally, make sure the call-to-action (CTA) link in your email is prominent, and obvious, and uses language that encourages users to take action. To be clear about the action you want email readers to take, you can also add a sizable CTA image or button underneath.

b. Email for Product Updates

Product emails are challenging. People prefer not to receive these frequently, and they are usually not as interesting or captivating as something like an email with an offer. Having said that, it's crucial to keep these emails short and to the point.

To keep their clients or fan bases informed about the newest features and functionalities, many businesses opt to send weekly or monthly product digests. And regardless of how much a customer adores your company, it still requires work on their part to teach them how to use new features or convince them that a new purchase is worthwhile.

Sending a sort of roundup of new updates or products regularly might be a better option than barraging your contacts with emails about each product update. For each update you list, use a strong headline, a clear summary, and an image showcasing the feature or product. It's crucial to link to a specific page for each feature so that readers can easily find out more about it.

c. Online newsletters or magazines

Do you update a corporate blog for your organization? Are you a newspaper or other media organization? Regardless of which of these categories you fall under, many businesses opt to send a compilation of recent news or articles that were published on a weekly or monthly basis. Furthermore, it's imperative to share these email roundups in a visually appealing manner if you want people to read them.

Use an image along with a headline, a succinct summary or introduction, and a CTA encouraging recipients to read more in these roundup emails. This straightforward format will enable you to feature multiple articles without sending an excessively long email while still allowing you to use visuals to draw readers to each one.

d. Invitation to Event

Email can be a fantastic tool for advertising a forthcoming event you're hosting. However, it's critical to make it abundantly clear why the event is worthwhile for their attendance if you want to invite your contacts and encourage them to sign up.

Visuals are a fantastic way to do this. Attending many events is expensive, with the majority costing quite a bit. So, if you want to get more registrations, cut back on the copy and convince people that the event will be fantastic.

e. Specific Email

You might occasionally want to address a specific email to a particular group of people. For instance, if you're hosting a conference or event, you might want to send a special email to attendees only to inform them of any updates to the event that they should be aware of. Alternatively, if your company is community-based, it might be a good idea to welcome all of your new members in a monthly email.

f. Co-marketing Email

When two or more similar businesses collaborate on a task, event, or other promotion that benefits both parties, it is known as "co-marketing." Co-marketing is primarily attractive because it allows you to broaden your reach by using another company's audience.

Sometimes the connection results in a strategic announcement, and other times it is as straightforward as hosting a webinar together.

Let's use the latter as an illustration of how co-marketing emails operate and the advantages they provide: Consider that you and another business partner want to host a webinar together on a specific topic. Due to this, the webinar will probably be promoted to the email lists of both of your businesses (pending your agreements). One of the primary advantages of co-marketing alliances is exposure to a list that is not your own.

Make it clear in the emails your company sends that this promotion or occasion is the result of a collaboration with business A, especially if your co-marketing partner is particularly well-known or impressive. You can accomplish this by changing your email's company logo to incorporate the other company's logo as well. Additionally, make sure your copy mentions both companies and creates a unique graphic or image to help the reader visualize the promotion or event.

g. Internal Updates

Keep in mind that your employees are a very important audience for your business. To keep their staff informed of the most recent company information, including new product updates, marketing offers, or events, many businesses, particularly those that are larger, choose to send internal updates or newsletters.

Less beauty and more clarity are important in these emails. The most crucial formatting advice for these kinds of emails is to arrange the information in a clear and practical manner. Once your formatting is perfect, all that's left to do is highlight the information that matters most for each offer or update so that everyone can clearly understand what it's saying.

3. Reach Site Summary (RSS) Newsletter
You can send a specific kind of letter to your subscribers who signed up for your newsletter through your blog by integrating your email service provider with your website. It is also referred to as the "Blog Newsletter." Customers can easily access updates and a curated selection of content via an RSS feed, and RSS is a simple way to syndicate your company's content on other websites.

A feature called RSS-to-email combines RSS feeds and email subscriptions. As a business owner, this enables you to send emails with updates and recently posted blog content. Additionally, you can send periodic RSS-to-email newsletters that provide a summary of blog content those subscribers may have missed rather than sending an email every time a blog is published, which may annoy your subscribers.

Once you've decided on an RSS feed, established a schedule, and decided on an audience, you can add an email to it. A saved segment can be chosen, a new segment can be made, or you can add your entire audience to an RSS campaign.

Tips for using RSS feeds

The quickest way to use RSS is to start by following your favorite blogs, but that's just one of the many advantages it provides. Here are four strategies for using RSS feeds to automate your tasks and gather the information you care about.

a. Keep up with new YouTube channel uploads, podcasts, and blog posts.

RSS can be used for purposes other than just reading blogs. Additionally, you can use it from within your RSS reader to access new episodes of podcasts and videos that have been uploaded to your preferred YouTube channels. In many cases, subscribing to an RSS feed for any kind of content only requires pasting the URL of the page you want to follow into your RSS reader (for example, the homepage of a blog, a podcast episode list, a YouTube channel homepage, etc.). You can immediately subscribe to an RSS feed if one is available for that page.

b. Subscribe to and view email newsletters in your RSS reader.

XML feeds are created from any newsletters that are sent to that email address. Simply add the provided feed link to your RSS reader to view those newsletters. After that, you won't have to worry about newsletters clogging up your email inbox because they will appear alongside the other content you follow in your RSS reader along with the newsletters you want to read.

c. Auto-generate email newsletters.

RSS is a fantastic tool for staying up to date with the content that your favorite publishers are posting, but it also functions admirably from the opposite perspective. You can automatically create email newsletters if you're a publisher by using an RSS feed for your blog, podcast, YouTube channel, social media profile, etc.

You can use RSS to push information to your email newsletter tool rather than manually copying and pasting it, for instance, if your newsletter contains a list of your most recent posts with titles, links, and summaries.

d. Keep track of brand mentions in a feed.

To track brand mentions online, you could pay a monthly subscription fee for a brand monitoring tool, but you can accomplish the same task for nothing by using RSS feeds and a reader. If you've set up Google Alerts for your name or the name of your company, you can have the alerts sent to an RSS feed rather than an email address. You can obtain the link required to subscribe to the feed in your RSS reader when configuring your alert.

The advantages of RSS feeds

As social media became more popular, RSS began to lose popularity. The best way to stay updated on brands' and authors' new content, however, isn't to follow them on social media. One example is that some companies post links to both new and archived content every fifteen minutes of every day. There's no guarantee that among all of the clutter in your feed, you'll just happen to notice new content. Second, social media platforms rarely display all of the content posted by the accounts you follow.

As an alternative, they employ algorithms that determine what you want to see and surface that content first. You usually won't get to see everything if that's what you want to see.

Contrarily, RSS feeds present all of the content that has been posted to the websites you follow, all in reverse chronological order.

There is no algorithm for selecting what you should or shouldn't see; no outdated content is included in the list, and no content is repeated. Social media is your best option if you primarily want to see content that lots of people have liked or engaged with. However, RSS always outperforms social media if what you want to see is all of the most recent content from the websites and people you care about.

Chapter 5

Autoresponders

They are electronic newsletters that are programmed to be sent out immediately following a contact's list subscription. You can write several messages to be sent out sequentially in a cycle. They aid in campaign automation and recipient-specific management of communication. They can be sent sequentially or periodically, beginning the day a contact subscribes to your list.

For instance, you could create an autoresponder program that:

a. An immediate welcome message from your company is sent to anyone who joins your mailing list.

b. After a week, they get coupon codes for some of your products.

c. They get a social media follow-up invitation two weeks later, and so on.

The significance of autoresponders

The use of autoresponders significantly improves your email marketing. If autoresponders are configured properly, subscribers will receive relevant messages from your company at the appropriate times without you having to worry about manually sending these out. Therefore, it is clear that saving you tons of time is the main advantage of autoresponders.

However, if you use autoresponder emails strategically, they can also bring in a substantial amount of money for your company.

Guidelines for sending autoresponders

The following recommendations are for sending autoresponders:

1. Keep it in check

If there isn't a very good business reason to send your subscribers a lot of emails in quick succession, keep the gaps between your email autoresponders fairly long.

2. Maintain relevance

Make use of the details your subscriber provided during the sign-up process to direct them to content that they are most likely to find interesting. If a subscriber previously expressed interest in Product A, take caution before adding them to a cycle about a very unrelated product, such as Product B.

3. Always send pertinent content

As soon as you've created an email autoresponder campaign, go through each email you've added to it and make sure it offers something of value to your subscribers (whether it's in the form of insightful content or an alluring offer). If not, think about taking it out of the cycle.

4. Don't just 'drip' - implement marketing automation

Since the earliest "drip campaigns," which were time-based drip campaigns, autoresponders have advanced significantly. Today, you can build incredibly complex user journeys that maximize revenue by using a wide range of marketing automation triggers, including opens, clicks, website visits, and purchases.

5. Make sure the information on your sign-up forms for mailing lists is accurate.

You need the right information to maximize the effectiveness of autoresponders. Find out what you need to do to create the best autoresponder cycle for your company. You might need to collect information on a person's location, date of birth, interests, etc. Always try to keep autoresponders firmly in mind when designing your data capture forms!

6. Know the laws governing data protection

It's more crucial than ever to abide by data protection laws in the age of the General Data Protection Regulation (GDPR) and the California Consumer Privacy Act (CCPA). Be very conscious of your responsibilities in this regard, make sure you always have explicit consent before including any subscribers in autoresponder cycles and provide users with a simple way to unsubscribe from your mailing list.

Chapter 6

Email Deliverability

Email deliverability describes what happens after the message is acknowledged by the receiving email server. For instance, whether an email is put in the inbox, spam folder, or somewhere else will determine its deliverability status.

Email delivery is crucial, especially when sending important emails for a business such as password resets, status updates, and urgent alerts. This is because if the emails end up in the spam folder, neither you nor your customers will find them useful.

Now that you are aware of what "delivery" generally means, let's examine the circumstances under which an email is considered to have been "delivered." Email deliverability is more directly related to inbox placement. If you are having trouble getting your emails to the inbox, the following best practices can help. An email is considered delivered when:

1. The receiving mail server acknowledges the email.

In this instance, the message is successfully received by the mail server after leaving the sender's mail client. The receiving mail server must still put forth more effort to determine how to manage the message properly. This situation is comparable to mailing a package to an office building's mailroom. It doesn't necessarily follow that the intended recipient received the package even if someone signs off on it.

2. The message is delivered to the correct mailbox on the receiving mail server.

In this case, the message was not only received by the mail server but was also delivered to the right mailbox. As we mentioned earlier, this is comparable to sending a package to a mailroom, having someone sign the package, and then delivering the package to the intended recipient. However, in this instance, it is not known whether the recipient read the message.

3. The message is opened and read by the recipient.

In this instance, the assertion that the recipient opened and read the message pushes the notion of "when is an email considered delivered?" to its logical conclusion. The beauty of email is that it ends up in the inbox, so it would be greatly appreciated if you took every precaution to ensure that every email you sent to your subscribers ended up in their inbox so that they would read it.

Visit "GlockApps" to check the deliverability of your emails. It checks the email's delivery to the inbox and its spam score. Both ActiveCampaign and MailChimp's email marketing platforms are fully compatible.

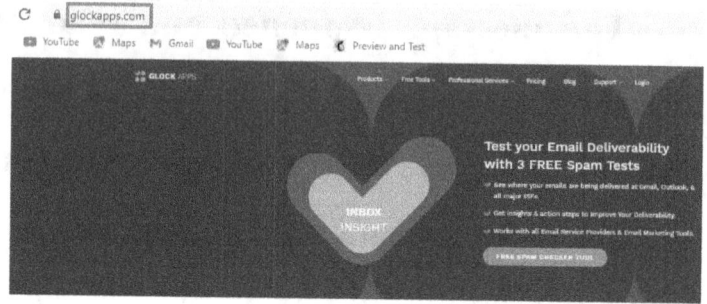

Factors Affecting Your Email Deliverability

1. Engagement of subscribers

A well-designed email attracts customers and, according to research, has the potential to improve conversion rates. The background of your email newsletter is part of what entices your subscribers. For your newsletter, use a matching background color, ideally one that goes with your company's branding. Your list will likely grow as a result of this.

2. Restricting negative metrics

A strong CTA button must be added to the email's content if your subscribers must click through to a website while reading it. This is just one example of the crucial metrics that can improve your email delivery rate.

3. Authentication

Experience has shown that customer reviews have an impact on delivery rates. If you're sending a newsletter to your subscribers about your goods or services, try to include reviews from previous customers to reassure them that what they're about to buy has received positive feedback.

4. Content

Email deliverability and open rates are better when the content is meaningful and organized well. Again, personalizing your content is advised. If at all possible, add your company or brand's signature at the end of your newsletter. Good content produces positive outcomes, favorable feedback, and excellent deliverability.

Chapter 7

Marketing Automation

Customer relationship management (CRM) and customer experience management (CXM) are subsets of marketing automation, which is focused on the definition, segmentation, scheduling, and tracking of marketing campaigns. Marketing automation increases the efficiency of tasks that would have been done manually and opens the door to new processes. Marketing automation is the process of using technology to automate various repetitive tasks that are carried out frequently in a marketing campaign.

Through the use of a single tool, marketing automation platforms enable marketers to manage intricate omnichannel marketing strategies while automating and streamlining client communication. Lead generation, lead segmentation, lead nurturing and scoring, relationship marketing, cross-sell and upsell, retention, and marketing ROI measurement all greatly benefit from marketing automation. To comprehend the impact and preferences of the customer, effective marketing automation tools use data from a separate or integrated CRM.

The Advantages of Marketing Automation

The advantages of implementing marketing automation include the following:

1. Reduces time

The time spent on manual tasks can be cut down by marketers using automation. such as content distribution and email follow-ups.

2. Lowers the cost of staff

The use of automation tools increases the effectiveness of marketing personnel and frees them up to concentrate on high-impact activities like creating marketing campaigns. Enhancing operational effectiveness can boost ROI.

3. Scales up operations

You can scale campaign operations with the aid of marketing automation as your customer base expands. Automating marketing procedures helps you reach and keep track of all customers as conversion rates rise.

4. Enhancing the connection between marketing and sales

The more prospects marketing generates, the greater the opportunities for purchases. The revenue of the company benefits from a rise in conversions. Additionally, by streamlining asset management, it is made sure that the sales division always receives the most recent version of the content that has been approved. As a result, brands become consistent.

5. Operations are centralized

Marketing automation tools arrange data and activities around a central hub. Systems for managing digital assets can be used, for instance, to build a dashboard and central repository. These allow you to share and manage rich media assets with ease.

6. Makes it easier to understand the behavior of your audience

You can gather more information about your visitors by utilizing marketing automation. A better understanding of your target customer can be achieved by collecting more specific data. The target market can then be divided into more manageable categories.

7. Enhances the experience of the customer

You can improve the shopping experience for your visitors by sending them highly customized campaigns. For instance, you can send emails based on patterns of behavior. Receiving an email recommending these products can enhance the user experience because customers respond better to personally relevant content.

The Disadvantages of Marketing Automation

There are some drawbacks to using marketing automation tools. Implementing them can be difficult for some businesses. Before implementing marketing automation tools, you might want to think about the following four factors:

1. Requires careful planning

You must be aware of any potential advantages the software may offer in advance. It's crucial to assess which processes can be automated and which cannot when thinking about automating your marketing operations.

2. It doesn't address inefficient processes

The new software won't immediately fix any problems or inefficiencies in your processes. You must make sure that the procedures are coordinated and that the teams work together. Although the marketing automation platform can make operations more efficient, it cannot address more serious problems. Before you start implementing solutions, you need to take the time to assess and improve the operational processes.

3. A steep learning curve

Every new software platform demands time and investment. The first few months can be challenging because the staff may have a steep learning curve. Your staff must be familiar with the new tools for processes to run smoothly.

The need for tool integration with the applications your employees frequently use should also be taken into account. You must carefully assess both your capacity for integrating tools and the time required to do so. Businesses that allow employees to bring their own devices, for instance, may experience difficulties integrating tools with those devices.

4. Message fatigue

Automation might encourage businesses to contact customers too frequently. As a result, customers may grow weary of the message.

PART B

ActiveCampaign >

Chapter 8

Introduction and Pricing Plans

With features for email marketing, lead scoring, and web analytics, in addition to a CRM platform and a live chat messaging platform called Conversations, ActiveCampaign offers cloud-based marketing and sales automation software. By including customer support in its services, it sets apart its software, known as "customer experience automation" (CXA), from conventional email marketing and CRM platforms. More than 850 applications are integrated by ActiveCampaign, such as Salesforce, WordPress, Shopify, PayPal,

Stripe, Gmail, Calendly, Slack, Facebook, and WooCommerce.

PC Magazine asserts that ActiveCampaign offers a ton of features for a fair price. The disadvantage is that even though there are many options for assistance, sometimes it can be challenging to use them. According to the solution review, "Users have access to thorough behavior tracking capabilities as well as precise marketing options through segmentation."

Marketing automation is among its key features. built-in integrations Conditional email content, contact tracking on the website or in an app, contact location tracking, Drag-and-drop email designer, intelligent autoresponders, newsletters, reporting for campaigns, contacts, and lists, Emails, SMS advertising, and real-time e-commerce data sophisticated segmentation and targeting of customized forms, automated series, Support is available via free phone, live chat, and email. Social media observation and response free private instruction, ASL-based contacts, sales automation, CRM, and free email templates.

ActiveCampaign is a collection of various marketing tools bundled into a user-friendly platform that is created to meet the requirements of various facets of small businesses. The system makes it possible to easily create beautiful and captivating emails, gathers more contact information, utilizes social media marketing, and, finally, makes marketing automation technology available to small businesses that were previously out of reach. More than 100,000 users rely on ActiveCampaign to help their businesses grow and use the system on a global scale. Without a credit card, the application can be quickly set up.

Pricing Plans

Instead of a free plan like Mailchimp, ActiveCampaign Conversations offers a 14-day trial with the same features as the Lite Plan.

> ➢ Marketing Automation
> ➢ Email Marketing
> ➢ Unlimited Email Sending
> ➢ Drag & Drop Email Builder

- ➤ 125+ Email Templates
- ➤ Send Newsletters
- ➤ Subscription forms
- ➤ Segmentation
- ➤ The site and Event Tracking
- ➤ Campaign and Automation Reporting

All of these features are available with a 14-day free trial if you have fewer than 500 contacts, and you can subscribe for $9 per month with 500 contacts for the Lite Plan and for $29 per month with 1,000 contacts. Your monthly budget will increase as your contact lists get bigger, which simply means that the price will depend on how many contacts you have and what features you want.

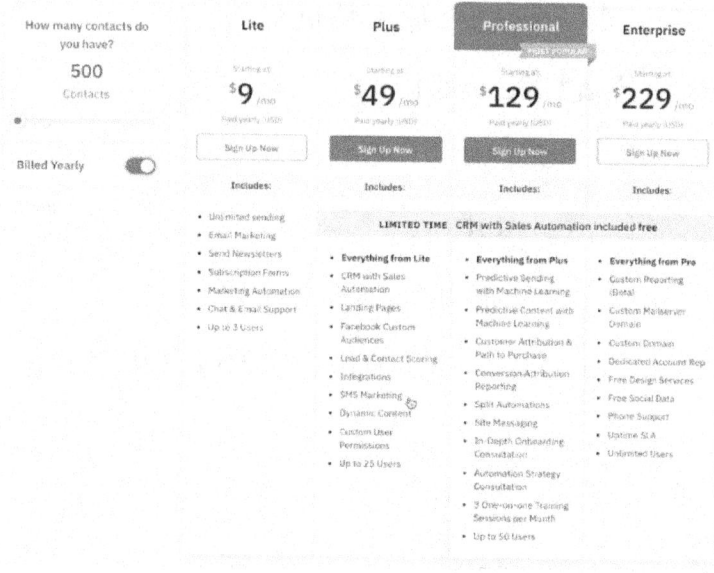

The annual plan at ActiveCampaign is discounted by 25%. Due to this, ActiveCampaign costs are very reasonable when compared to those of other marketing automation platforms.

Chapter 9

Lists

The most comprehensive segmentation method in ActiveCampaign, where you can create contacts, is called a list. Lists are therefore collections of contacts who have consented to receive communications from you. A "list owner" is a person or business that is the owner of a collection of names, numbers, addresses, or other data. This data may be rented or sold by a list owner to third parties, particularly for direct marketing uses.

You can further segment your lists with tags, and you can use custom fields to be even more specific and targeted than with tags. Contacts should be grouped together to form segments if they have similar behaviors and characteristics. Your lists should contain more contacts than any tag or custom field segment. This indicates that each list's distinguishing feature is very generic and shared by a large number of contacts.

Do you want to segment your audience? Use custom fields and tags instead of lists. However, the distinguishing feature of each tag is a little bit more particular and is shared by fewer contacts. The fewest number of contacts should be in segments defined by custom fields since these fields typically store information that is particular and private to each contact.

Note: *Messages and lists are connected in traditional email marketing. One message cannot be sent to contacts on different lists. Even if the content of the message is the same, you must create a different message for each list. ActiveCampaign, however, does not link messages to lists. In other words, you can send the same message to contacts who, despite being on separate lists, have a similar condition. This is made possible by automation as well as ActiveCampaign's general flexibility.*

Types of Lists

Subscribe and unsubscribe options are available for contacts in lists. On the "List" page of your account, as displayed in the screenshot below, you can create lists.

Add a List   ✕

List Name

eg. Monthly Newsletter, Sales Leads, etc.

List URL

http://

List Description

Remind your contacts why they are on this list. This will be viewable in emails
sent to this list.

                                    Cancel   Add

I'll only suggest that you think about using the main list and the customer list.

1. **Main List**: This list contains all of the tags and segments related to your prospects.

2. **Customer List:** This list is for the people you know who are customers. This list includes everyone who has purchased your product(s).

This straightforward method of handling lists is predicated on the idea that contacts are either leads or customers. Either you're attempting to convert them or you're attempting to upsell and nurture them. Simply choose your main list as the recipients if you need to send a one-time message to your prospects (and vice versa for customers).

How to create a list

- ❖ Go to the ActiveCampaign dashboard and select "Lists"

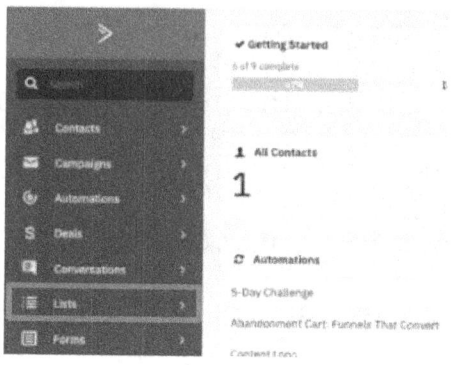

❖ Click the blue "Add a list" button located in the top-right corner of the list page.

❖ When a page appears, fill it out with your brand's credentials and press the "Add" button.

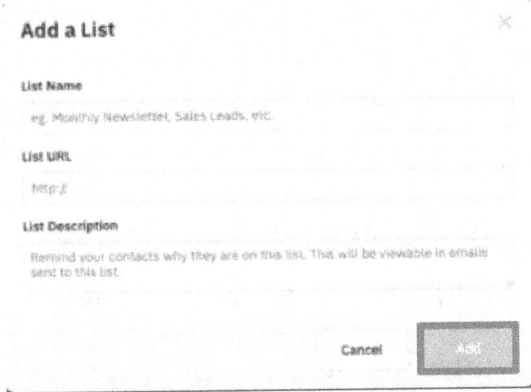

➤ **List Name:** Either the Main list or the Customer list.

➤ **List URL:** Your Website URL.

➤ **List Description:** Your contacts should understand exactly why they are on the list and why they chose to subscribe to that specific list. For instance, "You are receiving this email because you joined my website's mailing list (Main List)" or "You are receiving this email because you bought one of my digital products (Customer List)." You've now made a new list.

How to import contacts from a CSV file

After creating a list, you can use the Import tool to add contacts to your ActiveCampaign account from a CSV file. The Import tool allows you to map columns in your file to fields in your account, create new custom contact fields to map a column to, import contacts to a list, apply tags to the contacts, import contacts as active, unsubscribed, or excluded, and decide whether to update existing contacts as you import.

You can import your contacts from a CSV file by following the instructions:

❖ Go to the ActiveCampaign dashboard and select "Lists"

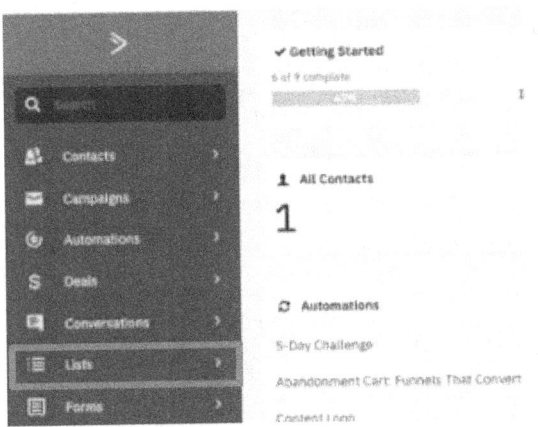

❖ Choose "Import contacts" from the list page's drop-down menu in the top-right corner of the screen.

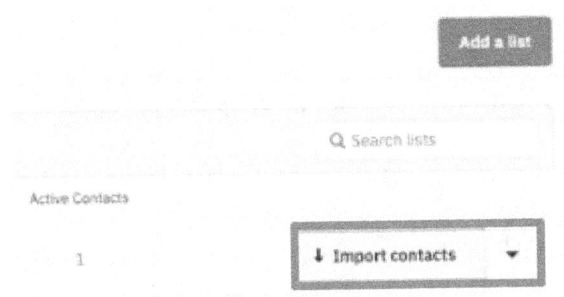

❖ You'll be directed to a page with two options: either import from a file or manually copy and paste your contacts.

Have existing contacts in a file? Import a .CSV file of your contacts or copy/paste your contacts for a quick import.

Import From File

Copy & paste your contacts

The best course of action is to upload the file into your ActiveCampaign list because the second option will be too complicated given that you might have over 1000 contacts. To do that, select the "Import From File" option.

❖ There will be a file browser displayed. Locate and select the file you want to import.

❖ After your file has been processed, the import screen will be displayed. By selecting the drop-down arrow next to each field, you can "Map the Columns in Your File to Fields in Your Account.

➢ Choose "Do Not Import This Field" if you don't want to import data from a particular column.

➢ Click "Add New Field" and adhere to the instructions to create a new field directly from the import page.

❖ Select any lists you want to add contacts to by scrolling down and clicking on them. Contacts can be added to various lists.

❖ Add tags (optional): You want to apply them to all contacts after they're imported.

Add tags (optional)

Tags allow you to identify your contacts. You could add a tag for how you obtained their information, whether they are a customer, etc.

As a best practice, you might want to add a tag that details where these contacts came from. If you need to later make any bulk edits to them, you can quickly locate them grouped this way.

❖ Choose "Import As Active Contact" from the drop-down menu after clicking the "Import Options" button.

Import options

| Import As Contact ▾ | ☐ Update existing contacts while importing |

The "Update existing contacts while importing" checkbox should be selected. This will search your account for an email address that matches and add any additional contact information from your file to the contact record.

❖ When you're done with the configuration settings, click the "Import Now" button in the bottom right corner of the page.

The size of the CSV file will determine how long it takes to import contacts.

When everything is done, you can see the number of contacts that were successfully imported.

Take note of the following:

1. Only CSV files are compatible with the import tool.

If you keep your contacts in a spreadsheet, be sure to export them as a CSV file before importing. Additionally, CSV files require proper formatting.

2. There must be an email address for each contact in your database.

ActiveCampaign will import the first instance of a contact with the same email address from your file and ignore any additional contacts with the same email address.

3. Contacts may be imported and added to "Active" automation.

Contacts will be added to the automation with the status "Active" If

a. A trigger for automation is used with the list you are adding them to.

b. You tag contacts for import and then use those tags as automation triggers,

c. A field's values are being imported and the trigger for the automation is using that field.

4. During the contact import process, it is not possible to designate an account owner.

ActiveCampaign will assign the default account owner to each account in your CSV file if it has an "Account" column.

Chapter 10

Forms

The best way to think about forms is as entry points to email lists. By filling out forms and submitting their information, contacts are added to your database. Your database would be inaccessible to potential contacts if there were no forms.

I'll discuss the applications for forms, important considerations to make when designing them, the meaning, advantages, and disadvantages of double opt-in, and how to build a form in ActiveCampaign.

What is the purpose of forms?

ActiveCampaign uses forms to:

1. Subscribe to your email list
2. Get a lead magnet
3. Obtain a quote

Form choices to keep in mind

1. If you want people to fill out the fields, make them mandatory.
2. Disable any blank fields and replace any data in existing fields.
3. Make sure to set your opt-in preferences; if you'd like, turn off double opt-in.
4. Send visitors to a welcome page
5. Hidden fields.
6. A form's appearance can be easily modified using CSS (optional).

Double Opt-in

A double opt-in is a two-step procedure a contact must go through before they are added to your list as an active contact. Contacts won't receive emails from you and won't be considered active contacts until they confirm.

The Advantages of Double Opt-in

1. It helps to make sure contacts want to hear from you.
2. After implementing double opt-in, contacts are more likely to open your emails.
3. Fewer spam complaints may help with deliverability.

4. It fulfills the requirements of a few countries or regions that demand a double opt-in process.
5. It helps prevent spam contacts from being added to your account as active contacts.

The disadvantages of double opt-in

1. The second step of your double opt-in process may not be completed by some contacts who do want to hear from you, so they won't receive your emails.
2. In comparison to using a single opt-in, your list might be a little bit smaller.
3. The conversion rate declines as a result.

Let's now discuss the procedures involved in creating a form in ActiveCampaign.

How to create a form

By clicking the green "+ New Form" button on the main form page, you can add a new form. By doing this, a "Create a new form" window is produced. Choose the type of form display you want to make, give your form a name, and specify any "form actions" you want ActiveCampaign to carry out each time a contact submits data to the form.

You can select from four different form display types: inline, floating box, modal pop-up, and floating bar. The image below shows how they are presented.

Note: *Only the inline form display is offered by the Lite plan. All other plans offer all four display modes.*

There is no restriction on the number of form actions you can add to each form; some examples are: tagging the contact, creating a deal and adding it to a particular pipeline and stage, notifying an employee of form submission, and adding a contact to a list.

How to edit a created form

You must first create and edit a form before posting it on your website. Form creation is only necessary for website owners. A landing page, which I will explain how to create and design, will be a better option if you don't have a website.

You can create and edit your form using the steps below:

❖ Click "Forms" in the menu on the left side of the ActiveCampaign dashboard.

❖ Select "Inline" from the four available form types. Give it a name, choose the list, and create a tag (optional) by clicking on "Add an action." Then, click on the "create" button.

❖ You'll be asked to use the form builder. You will have a page similar to this in your workspace where you can design your form.

Subscribe for Email Updates

Add a descriptive message telling what your visitor is signing up for here.

Full Name

Type your name

Email*

Type your email

Submit

Marketing by
ActiveCampaign ➤

You can find your form builder's settings on the right side of the page.

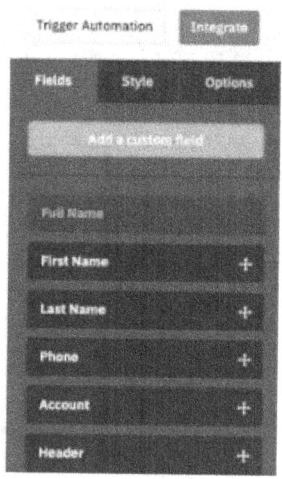

❖ Each block can be edited one at a time.
   The first step is to configure your
   thank-you page by making changes to
   the options on the form builder's right
   side. Click on the "option" button. By
   clicking on the drop-down arrow, you
   can switch the option from "Show

Thank You" to "Open URL," which will send website visitors to your customized thank-you page.

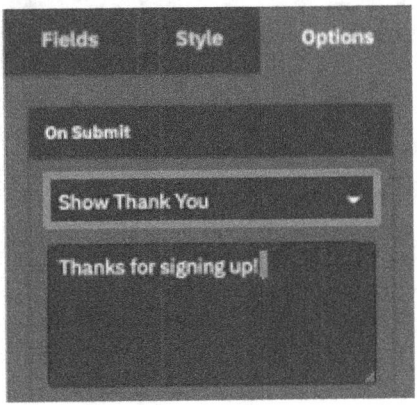

When you scroll down on the form action section, where you have already selected a list that you want your website visitors to subscribe to, To change the single or double opt-in option, click the "settings" button.

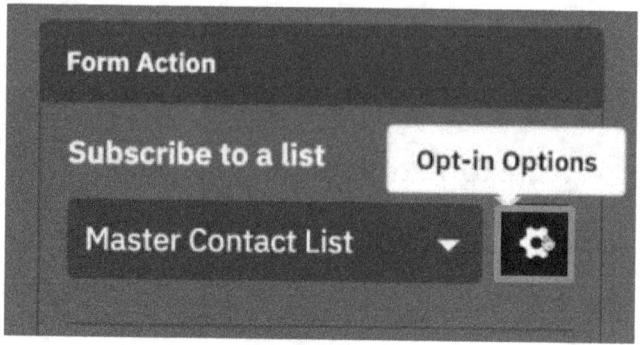

You'll be directed to a page that looks like this:

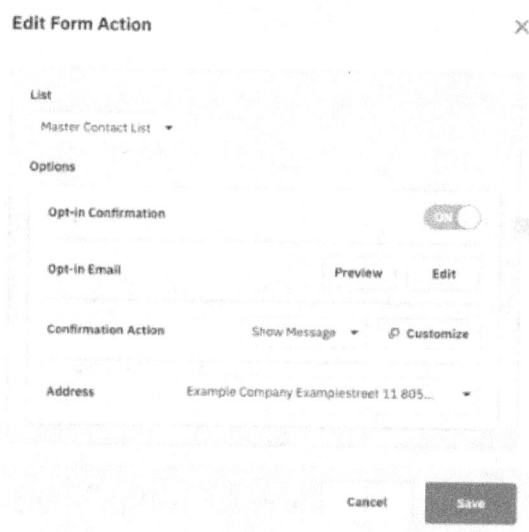

The additional confirmation form that visitors to your website must accept before becoming subscribers is disabled when you toggle off the opt-in confirmation button. It is known as "double opt-in." Click on "save"

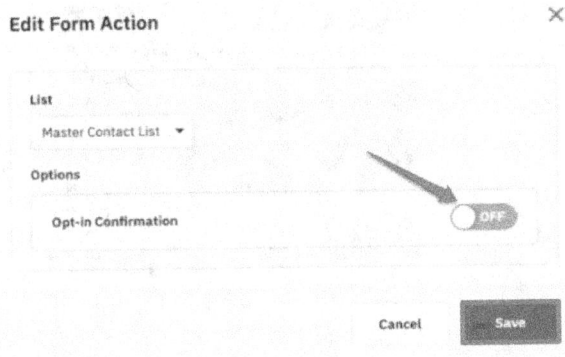

❖ By dragging and dropping any block of your choice from the settings on the right side of the page, you can edit or delete any field on your form.

However, email is a required field. Additionally, you can remove ActiveCampaign branding by selecting the "Style" button in the settings menu on the right side of the page. Turn off the "AC branding" button by scrolling down.

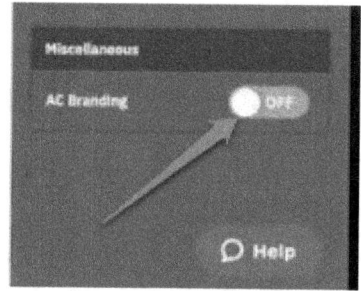

❖ Click on the "Full Name" field to edit it, then change the settings on the right side of the page.

By checking the box, you can also make it mandatory.

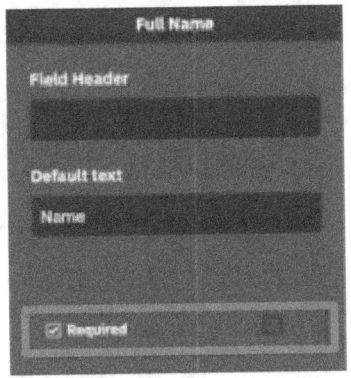

Your form will be affected by any setting adjustments you make.

❖ The fields you created earlier, such as name and email, can also be centered. In the settings, select "Style," then scroll down to "Custom CSS," and select the "Inspector" button.

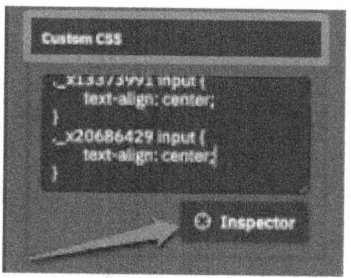

Click the field you want to center, then follow the steps in the step above for both Name & Email.

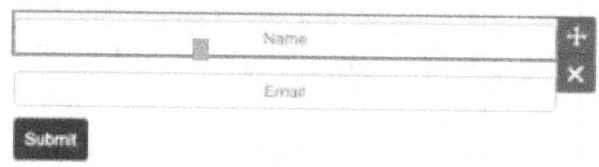

When you first click the "Inspector" button, it will automatically display "_submit{" on the workspace to the right after clicking the "Submit" button. Then, to adjust the field button, type something resembling the example below and press the "enter" button on your device to advance to the following line. The goal is to increase its width.

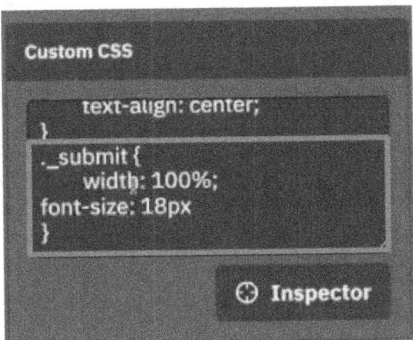

Once the setting is complete, you will have this.

If you want to change the background color, the paddling, the font sizes and width, and other things. To make the adjustments, click the "Style" button on the settings page.

❖ When you are done with the editing and design of your form, click on the "Integrate" button at the top-right corner of the page.

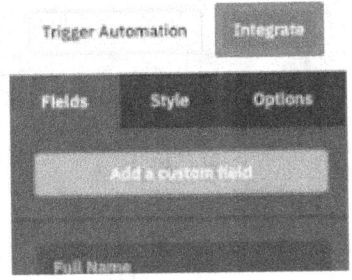

❖ For integrating your form, you have several options. Clicking the "embed" button on the page will allow you to integrate your website

Two options are available here:

➢ **Simple Embed**: This is a suggested option because any changes you make to your form in ActiveCampaign will automatically affect the embedded form on your website.

➢ **Full Embed**: For this type, any changes you make to your form in ActiveCampaign won't affect the form that is already embedded on your website.

Click the "Save and exit" button in the top-right corner of the page once the code installed on your website is complete.

Chapter 11

Landing Page

Using simple templates and ActiveCampaign Pages, you can quickly create stunning landing pages with high conversion rates. Your marketing campaigns can generate more leads, generate sales, and start automated processes by using landing pages.

You can build landing pages using the tool Pages to support your marketing campaigns. When someone clicks on a link from somewhere online, like a social media post, an advertisement, or an email, they "land" on a standalone web page known as a landing page.

The main purpose of landing pages is to persuade visitors to take an action on your page. This can involve doing things like:

a. Form submission.

b. A list subscription.

c. Making a purchase.

d. Downloading a pdf or other file.

e. Event Registration.

You can either create your landing page from scratch or use one of the provided premade templates. After choosing a template, you can further alter your layout using the drag-and-drop designer. Additionally, you can add Google Analytics code to your page and enable ActiveCampaign site tracking for it. When you're prepared to publish, ActiveCampaign will create a special URL for your page, which you can edit and include in the resources for your marketing campaign. People will land on your landing page the moment they click the link.

Customizing the landing page design

You can edit the theme and layout of your page as well as add content using the page builder. Page blocks are used for every page you make. You can construct and modify your page layout using these blocks.

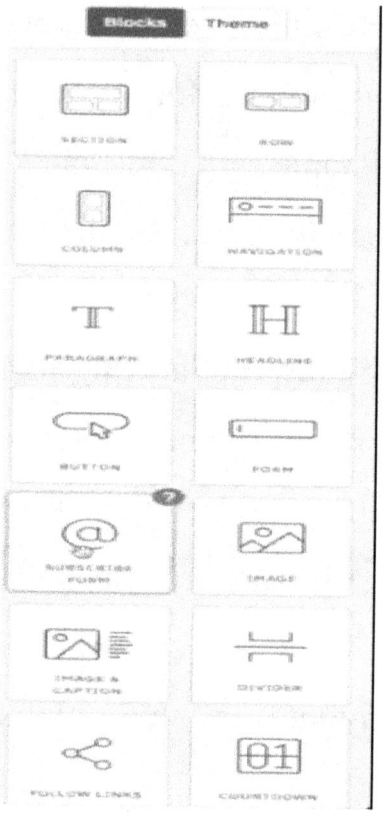

Drag a block from the right bar to where you want it in your layout to add it to your design. The block names and descriptions are shown in the table below.

Block Name	Block Description
Section	Create a section and add additional content blocks to it.
Row	Create a row for your page, and then additional blocks are added to it.
Column	A column is added to your page with additional blocks.
Navigation	Add navigation to your page to help users find their way around.

Text	Text can be added, modified, and styled.
Headline	Add a compelling headline to your page.
Button	Include a button that directs visitors to your website or allows them to download files.
Inline Form	Create or incorporate an ActiveCampaign form into your page.
Pages Form	Include a contact information collection form on your page.

Image	Include an image on your page.
Image and Caption	Include an image with a caption
Divider	Include a horizontal line on your page
Follow Links	Include social media icons on your page so that users can follow you there.
Countdown	Create a sense of urgency on your page by including a countdown clock.

Bulleted List	Add a list with bullets to your page.
Embed	Put some custom code on your page, such as an ActiveCampaign form.
Video	Include a video on your page.

Making a Landing Page

In the Pages section of your ActiveCampaign account, you can make landing pages. A page template is the first step in creating each page. The content of your page is initially organized based on the page templates you choose.

The simple steps for creating a landing page are provided below:

❖ Click on "Site" in the menu on the left side of the ActiveCampaign dashboard.

❖ On the secondary menu, click on "Pages." If this menu is collapsed, move your mouse pointer over the ActiveCampaign logo in the top left corner and click the arrows that appear to the right to expand it.

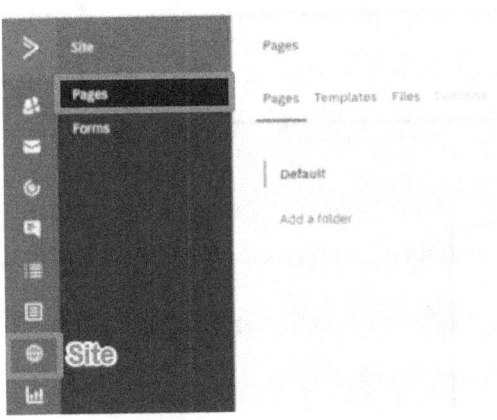

❖ Click the "Add a new page" button on the right side of the page as you are directed to a new page.

❖ The template page will open. Find the template you want to use for your page. The "Use This Template" option will appear when you move your mouse over the template. Select "Blank" if you prefer to start with a blank template.

Note: *Any template can be viewed before use. To do this, select the "Preview" option that appears when* *you hover your cursor over the template. On both a desktop and a mobile device, you can see how the template appears.*

❖ When the template loads in the page builder, a "Rename Page" modal window will show up. Click the "Save" button after entering the name of your page in the field provided.

Now that your landing page is ready for customization, you can add content to it.

Chapter 12

Newsletter

A newsletter is defined as a piece of writing that provides relevant information about a subject or group to a target audience. Email newsletters are a powerful tool for expanding your customer base and your business.

One of the most dependable marketing tactics for many companies is the publication of a regular newsletter. The following benefits of using newsletters are: increasing the size of your email list; driving repeat traffic to your website; converting subscribers into buyers; establishing your authority and trust in your field; and cultivating audience loyalty. Your newsletter, along with other forms of email marketing, can produce a predictable ROI that outperforms all other forms of advertising with the right strategy. You can share your best content, advertise limited-time offers, and cultivate a rapport with your ideal clients if you have access to your audience's inbox.

Strong email marketing strategies can be created in a variety of ways. You'll find a lot of value in sending a daily, weekly, or monthly newsletter, whether you're a solo creator starting a business outside of work hours or a large corporation looking to strengthen relationships with your contact list. To begin, here are some components that marketers typically include in newsletters:

a. Details that are pertinent to a subject or organization

b. Helpful hints or suggestions

c. Organizational or subject-specific news

d. A call to action

e. Details about existing or new products or services

There are various schools of thought regarding what makes a great newsletter, but the following fundamental principles apply to all well-known newsletters:

a. They have an excellent design.

b. Relevant and distinctive content and curation are provided.

c. They consistently provide the reader with value.

The various types of email design blocks

You can use email design blocks as building blocks to make email campaigns, automation emails, and email templates. They are accessible through the drag-and-drop email designer. The creation and customization of your email or email template can be done using any of these blocks.

The following are email design blocks with their respective descriptions:

Block Name	Description
Text block	Use this to insert text into your email or email template; after doing so, click on the text block to display the editing toolbar. The font, size, color, and alignment of your text can then be modified from there. Links and personalization tags are additional options.

	You can modify padding and margins, background color, line height (the distance between lines), and background color in the "Options" tab on the right.
Image	This can be used to include an image or animated gif in your email or email template. Moreover, you can

	edit any images you intend to include in your emails using the image editor.
Video	Use this to include a video link in your email. A screenshot from your video will be created by the block and displayed in your email along with a play button. Contacts can listen to

	your message when they receive it by clicking the play button in your email. Their browser will launch the video in a new tab or window.
Line break	The horizontal line break between your content blocks can be added with the help of this design element.
Spacer	Use this responsive design feature to

	include white space between your content blocks.
RSS feed	Utilize this to include your RSS feed in emails. You can quickly and easily automatically share news and brand-new blog posts with your contacts using this block.
Social Links	Put your social media links here and use them in your emails. By doing this, you'll

	enable recipients to share your message on their social networks.
HTML	You can use this to include unique HTML code in your email. For instance, you could use this to add a countdown timer.
Products	When you add this block to an automation email, it will show up as a design block. Keep in

| | mind that to use this block, your account must be configured with the Shopify Deep Data integration.

This block can display the following items for products in your connected Shopify store:
  ➢ Image
  ➢ Name
  ➢ Price
  ➢ Description
  ➢ Link to view |
| --- | --- |

	➢ The "Buy Now" button This email block is available on the Plus, Professional, and Enterprise Plan
Abandoned cart	It is exclusive to automation emails. When creating emails for any automation that makes use of the "Abandons Cart" trigger, this block will show up.

	This email block is available on the Plus, Professional, and Enterprise Plan.
Predictive contents	To increase your click-through rate, use this block to send the appropriate content to the appropriate contacts. This email block is available on the Plus, Professional, and Enterprise Plan.

Moving and Adding Email Design Blocks

Adding design blocks

It's simple to include design blocks in your email. Drag the desired block from the right menu onto your design to achieve this. There is a green highlight line that you can see as you drag the content block into your email. The content block will be positioned where this line indicates it will be when you release the design block.

Moving design blocks

A design block can be easily moved once it has been added to your email or email template. To act in that way:

❖ Your mouse should be over the block you want to move.

❖ To the right of the block, a four-directional handle will appear. Click it.

❖ The block can be moved by dragging it to the desired location.

Block settings for email designs

There are different settings for each design block in your email or template. The following settings are available for email design blocks:

Setting Name	Description
Duplicate	The block will be duplicated exactly if you choose this option. For predictive

	content, this is not available.
Make conditional	Based on segments, you can specify which recipients will see this block. For more details, see the help article titled "How to use conditional content." For predictive content, this is not available.
Hide on mobile devices	When the email is viewed on a mobile device, this option

	will make the block invisible.
Save to content library	You can use this option to save the block to a content library. You can quickly include it in any email or template you make after saving it. For predictive content, this is not available.
Delete this	By selecting this option, the block will

	be eliminated from your design.

To gain access to a design block's settings:

> ➢ Navigate to the block with your mouse.
> ➢ The gear icon that appears should be clicked.

The design block's "option" menu for email Each design block has its own distinct set of styles, but each block also has a common set that you can edit in the right-hand menu's "Options" tab. By clicking any block in your layout, this menu will be displayed.

Option Name	Description
Block background	Use this to change the color of a single block's background.
Block border	Borders can be widened or narrowed by changing their pixel value. You can choose the border style (solid or dot) and border-radius as you change the border's pixel size. Additionally, you have the option of selecting a border

	color.
Block margin	Margin values are predetermined as pixels and can be changed. Additionally, you can decide which sides will have margins.
Block padding	Padding is predetermined as a pixel value and is adjustable. Additionally, you can decide which sides will be padded.

Column background	Use this to give a column's background some colors.

Chapter 13

Email Automation

No matter your level of experience with marketing automation, I will walk you through the steps to create automation from scratch. You can use the steps as a manual or as step-by-step instructions to build automated workflows by combining different triggers, actions, and logic. These fundamental actions must be taken into account when creating new automation:

❖ Go to the Automation Overview page by selecting "automation" from the left menu.

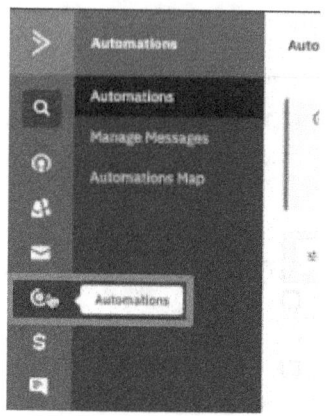

❖ On the left side of the page, click "Create an automation." You'll see an automation window.

❖ Click "Continue" after selecting "Start from Scratch."

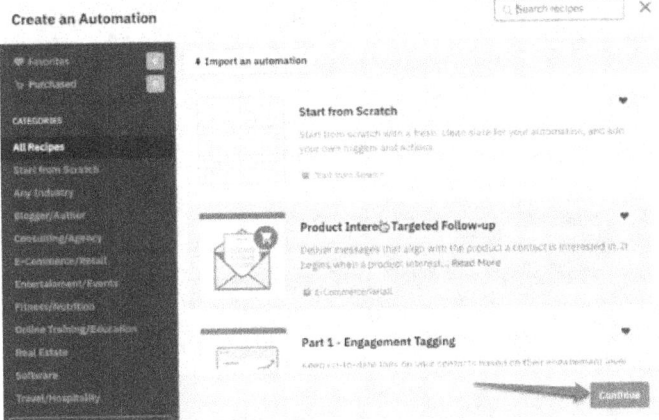

Including a start trigger

In this section, I'll go over how to start this automation whenever someone is added to a list. To configure that:

❖ Select "Subscribes to a list" from the trigger options.

❖ You'll see a modal window. Next, select the list from the drop-down that will trigger the automation. I'll select

"Master Contact List" for this
illustration.

Action options (Contact subscribes to a list)   ×

Select list   Any list   ▾

Runs   On: Q Search lists

ADVANCED   ✓ Any list

Segmer   Master Contact List   automation

Back   Add Start

Instead of having a different trigger for
each form, it makes sense to start this
automation whenever someone is
added to the master list since multiple
forms may be used to add people to it.

❖ Make sure this trigger action is set to
run "once" to prevent contacts from
restarting this automation and getting

the same message repeatedly. (This choice ought to be the default selection)

"Runs once" denotes that a contact will only ever enter your automation through a single trigger, regardless of how frequently they satisfy the trigger conditions.

"Runs multiple times" denotes the fact that a contact will always enter your automation through a particular trigger, regardless of how frequently they satisfy the triggering requirements. Click the "Add Start" button to complete configuring this trigger.

Sending a welcome email

The best practice is to send a welcome email to a new contact as soon as they opt into your list. Welcome emails frequently have some of the highest open and click-through rates, so take advantage of this opportunity to get crucial messages in front of your contacts and highlight crucial calls to action.

❖ Select "Send Email" from the "Add New Action" modal's list of actions. As soon as you have finished configuring your "Subscribes to List" start trigger, this modal will show up.

❖ You'll see a modal window. Click the "create an email" link.

❖ Afterward, enter the email's name in the corresponding field. Then, click the "Create" button.

Contacts won't see this internal email name because it is private. I advise choosing a name that is clear and will serve to remind you of the email's objective. Keep in mind that you can later give the email a subject line that recipients will see.

Create a New Email   ✕

Email Name (This will not be visible to your contacts.)

Welcome Email: Youtu

                                                    Cancel   Create

❖ After that, you will be taken to the "Templates" page where you can choose the email template type. Select the type of template you want to use, then click "Continue."

❖ Next, you get to decide which template you want to use. Hover your mouse over a template to select it, then click the "select" button.

❖ When you locate the template that best serves your needs, mouse over it and select it.

❖ It will display a "Sender Details" modal. From this page, you can edit the email's sender details and add a subject line. What you create at this stage is not final because you can access and edit these options later.

Customizing the welcome email

❖ The email designer will launch. Blocks of your email are separated and can be moved around.

❖ Drag a block to the sidebar, hold it there until the desired position is highlighted, and then release it to add it.

❖ Drag your mouse over a block, click the gear icon, and then select "Delete this" to remove it.

❖ Several formatting options will show up above a block when you click on it as well as in the right sidebar. Spend some time learning about each block type and the options available to you, because different block types have different options.

❖ Click the "Next" button in the top-right corner of the screen after customizing the text and formatting the email. You'll be taken to the "Campaign Summary" page.

Review the Campaign Summary page.
You can learn the following from the "Campaign Summary":

❖ Check or make changes to the message's sender information, subject, preheader text, and name.

❖ Activate or deactivate "Open/Read Tracking"

- ❖ Set "Link Tracking" to on or off.

- ❖ Activate or deactivate "Google Analytics" tracking

- ❖ Email yourself or other team members as a test recipient.

- ❖ check out message previews

- ❖ View notifications of possible problems with your campaign that could set off spam filters

- ❖ Switch the "Reply tracking" button from "off" to "on" if you included a call-to-action in your email. As a result, you can use the response to learn more about how your contacts are engaging with you and the campaign's effectiveness.

Options		
Open/Read Tracking ❶	0 Automation(s)	ON
Link Tracking ❶	Customize	ON
Reply Tracking ❶		OFF
Google Analytics ❶		OFF

❖ At the top of the page, click the "Finish" button.

Including a "Wait" condition

To separate the contacts going through this automation, I want to use an "If/Else" condition. I want them to be tagged as having opened the email if they did. I want to tag them in that way if they clicked the email's link. Additionally, I want to tag them appropriately if they didn't open it or click a link. However, I can't just add the "if/else" because that would send the email and then check to see if anyone opened or clicked it right away. Nobody would have the time to even open it! Because of this, "wait" conditions are very helpful. They enable you to delay the automation until your contacts have ample opportunity to engage in the desired behavior.

In this instance, I'll give contacts a week to respond to the email, but I'll use a "Wait until..." condition to have the automation start once they've clicked the link.

To include a Wait action:
- ❖ On the right menu, click "Conditions and Workflow."

❖ Move the "Wait" action under the "Send email" action.

❖ You will be given the option to choose between waiting for a specific amount of time or until certain conditions are met after adding the "Wait" condition. Remember that if you select "Wait... until specific conditions are met," you still have the option to set a time limit. For example, you could say, "Wait seven days OR until the link in the email is clicked, then start the automation."

The best choice, in this case, is "wait... until specific conditions are met," because you can begin the automation as soon as the desired behavior has been attained.

Add a Wait Condition ✕

Wait for a specified period of time

Wait until specific conditions are met

❖ Clicking "Wait until specific conditions are met" will bring up the Conditions Editor, where you can specify the conditions your contacts must satisfy. The two conditions I'm using are "Actions > Has opened" in the "Welcome Email: YouTube" or "Action > Has clicked on a link" in the "Welcome Email: YouTube," and I'm selecting "Any link" that I used in the email.

Conditions Editor ✕

Wait until the following conditions are met:

Has opened	-	Welcome Email: Youtube
And **Or** Has clicked on a link	-	Welcome Email: Youtube Any link ✕

+ Add another condition

Add a New Segment Group

Cancel   Save

Click "Save" once you've finished setting your condition.

❖ You will now be prompted to specify the amount of time that contacts should hold off if they have not yet opened the email or clicked the link. Usually, two days are sufficient to respond to an email. If they haven't at that point, I will assume that they aren't particularly interested and that the message has been pushed so far down in their inbox that they might never see it.

Click "No time limit" to reveal the "Up to" option, click "Up to" to specify the duration of the delay, and then click the "Save" button. Depending on what makes the most sense to you, you are free to change that time up or down.

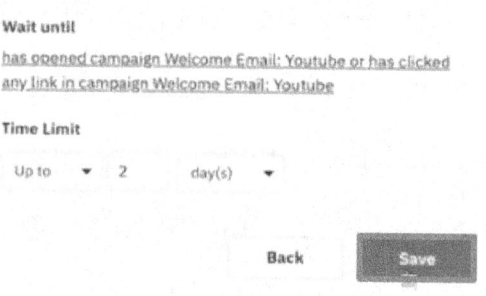

Including "If/Else" conditions

After giving your contacts enough time to respond to the message you sent them, let's categorize them based on what they did and did not do and assign tags that we can use to launch additional automation, develop segments, and carry out analytics.

❖ To add an "If/Else" action, click the "+" button beneath the "wait" action or drag and drop it from the sidebar.

❖ A modal window will appear asking you "How would you like to split this automation?" The interface you used to create the "Wait until..." conditions will be used to specify the conditions as well.

How would you like to split this automation? ✕

Has opened   —   Welcome Email: Youtube

And **Or** Has clicked on a link ˅   Welcome Email: Youtub   Any link

+ Add another condition

Add a New Segment Group

Cancel   Add

I chose "Any link" in the split action builder and set my conditions to "Actions > Has opened" or "Action > Has clicked on a link" in "Welcome Email: YouTube." Click "Add" to save the conditions. The automation for the setup above is shown below:

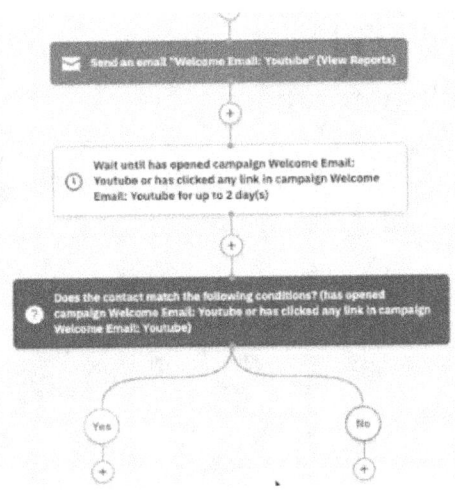

Keep in mind that the "if" or "else" action splits your automation.

❖ Your contact will take the "Yes" or "No" path depending on whether the conditions you set are met.

In the "No" path, I will send them another email with the same content but a different subject and a second condition that is analogous to the first one I set for them.

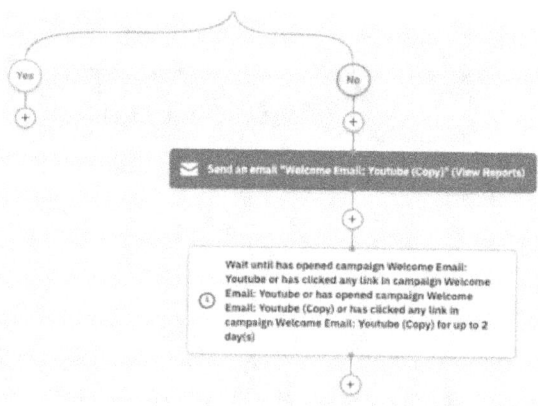

I also extended the time limit by two days. I then clicked the "Save" button.

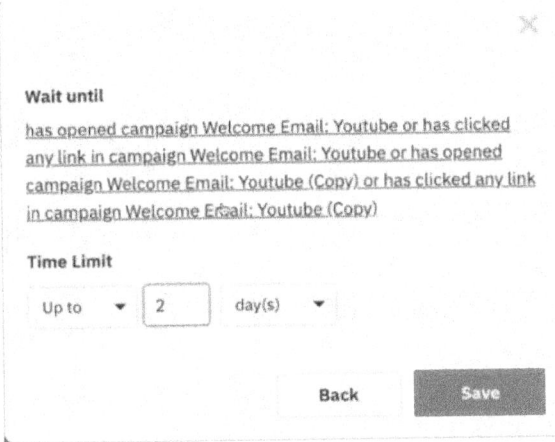

Wait until

has opened campaign Welcome Email: Youtube or has clicked any link in campaign Welcome Email: Youtube or has opened campaign Welcome Email: Youtube (Copy) or has clicked any link in campaign Welcome Email: Youtube (Copy)

Time Limit

Up to ▼ | 2 | day(s) ▼

Back   Save

❖ Next, I will redirect this group from the "no" path to the "yes" path. I'll create a 1-day delay and wait until 10 a.m. for them to receive the email before I do that. I will create a new email once these conditions have been established.

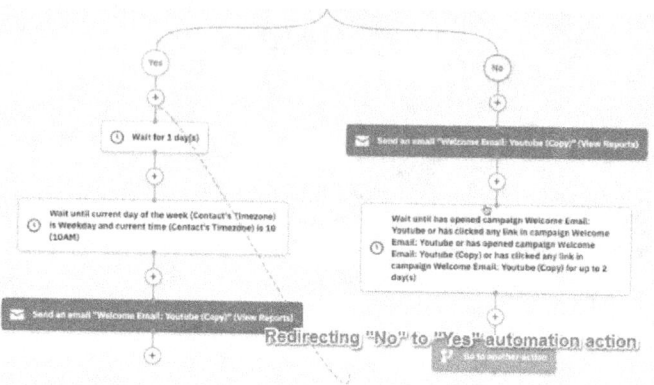

Redirecting "No" to "Yes" automation action

We now have an automation that sends a welcome email and/or an incentive for opting in as soon as someone subscribes to our list. We configure various time delays so that changes will be available for our contacts to read those unread emails in their inbox based on how they interact with those emails. You could send them a reminder email that encourages them differently if they haven't yet made a purchase or moved further down your sales funnel.

This allows you to build automation that uses information gathered from other automation to build a follow-up that changes based on the actions of your contact.

Finally, you could include an action to raise your contact's score as they respond to your messages to enhance the automation you've set up. If recipients open emails and click on particular calls to action, you could raise your contact or lead score for that recipient.

Send different follow-up emails to those who didn't open the email and those who didn't click the link. This shouldn't contain the same information because it will irritate your contacts.

Furthermore, you shouldn't keep pursuing them until they comply with your requests. It's pretty obvious that they aren't interested if you've given them two or three chances to respond, so you'd be better off not contacting them than pestering them and racking up SPAM complaints and low email interaction rates (which many email service providers take into account when determining deliverability).

Conclusion

Businesses with a dedicated email marketing team or an individual with the time to become familiar with the dashboard and create campaigns from scratch should use ActiveCampaign as their platform. The starter plan is incredibly cost-effective, the backend is jam-packed with features, and the extensive automation and analytics allow you to test and optimize your campaigns for success.

Users were impressed by the automation and analytics features of ActiveCampaign, which they rated as the best value email marketing platform. It didn't perform well in terms of design, and the absence of transactional emails renders it inappropriate for e-commerce businesses.

Last but not least, ActiveCampaign is preferred over other email marketing platforms due to its high deliverability rate, which increases the likelihood that your emails will reach your subscribers' primary inboxes.

PART C

GetResponse

Chapter 14

Introduction and Pricing Plans

GetResponse is a tool for online campaigns and email marketing. Online campaigns are created and maintained to achieve various corporate objectives. In a nutshell, campaigns that use GetResponse include:

➤ Acquiring leads

➤ Creation of email lists

➤ Sending and automating email, and

➤ Promoting goods

The following are a few intriguing GetResponse statistics and facts:

- ➤ More than 350,000 people use GetResponse.
- ➤ 27 languages are offered
- ➤ Over 300 active workers
- ➤ 16,000 websites are currently using the tool.
- ➤ $50 million was the estimated yearly income for the previous year.

Signup forms, landing pages, and webinars can all be used to generate leads with GetResponse. You create Facebook ads and send newsletters and automated emails. Analyze everything with reporting and analytics. With the complete suite of sales funnel tools from GetResponse, you can even design websites. With the drag-and-drop editor, the process seems easy. Drag the element you want to use onto your content, such as text, video, a button, or an image. To make it simple for you to create the content you want, GetResponse provides pre-built templates.

One of the most widely used platforms for email marketing is GetResponse. It functions as a lead generation, leads nurturing, and sales platform. Emails, forms, and automation workflows can all be made using GetResponse. GetResponse is well-equipped to handle these tasks.

Customers of GetResponse come from various industries and sizes of businesses. However, it appeals particularly to clients in the following groups:

1. Solopreneurs

For solopreneurs who manage multiple tasks at once, GetResponse is a good fit. A solopreneur must complete many tasks quickly and effectively. GetResponse is the ideal tool for these requirements.

The automation tools make it possible for one-person businesses to automate their email marketing.

2. Small to Medium Sized Businesses

Simple and quick-to-implement online marketing tools are preferred by small businesses. It makes sense to contrast GetResponse with high-end marketing tools for businesses. The functionality provided by GetResponse is comparable, but it is less expensive and simpler to use.

And don't forget that GetResponse provides hundreds of templates that are pertinent to expanding businesses. As a result, selecting GetResponse is easy. It makes it simple to expand your business.

3. E-commerce businesses

If you operate an online store, GetResponse could be of great help to you. GetResponse is used to generate traffic, gather customer information, send promotional emails, thank customers, and make online ads to advertise to new audiences.

You can complete the majority of your marketing tasks using GetResponse. How useful is that?

Pricing Plans

The email marketing platform from GetResponse offers four different pricing tiers: Basic, Plus, Professional, and Enterprise. An example of a basic plan with a list of 1,000 contacts and a 30-day free trial can be seen below. The list of 500 contacts will be reduced when you select the drop-down arrow to display the free plan.

As soon as you sign up for the free plan, You will receive the GetResponse forever-free plan, in addition to almost all of its features, for one month. The following are some features of the free plan:

➢ Email marketing

➢ Website Builder

➢ A list of 500 contacts

➢ Contact forms

➢ Sign up pages

Customer service, live chat, integrations, and marketing automation features are included with all plans, even the free GetResponse version.

Chapter 15

Lists

Your subscribers' contact information and email addresses are listed in the list.

How to import your contacts list

Before you begin:

a. Verify that your list complies with all import requirements, including those related to file size, file format, and data formatting. By doing this, you can be sure that the contents of your file will successfully upload to your contact list.

b. Make sure your list is of high quality. Real email addresses are not permitted to be included.

c. Before importing the file, request consent from individuals to add them to your contact list. There is only one opportunity for imports.

Now, adhere to these instructions to import contacts into GetResponse:

❖ Click the "Add contacts" button under "Lists" to add contacts. A fresh page loads.

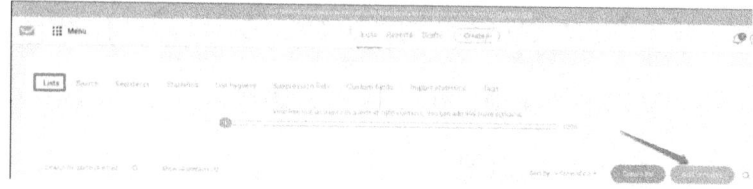

❖ Select the list from the drop-down menu. If you want the contacts to begin receiving autoresponders, choose "Add to autoresponder cycle." Choose the day of the cycle you want to add the contacts to next.

❖ To choose how to add contacts, click "Upload a file, use an external service, or paste rows." From there, you can choose if you want to:

    a. upload a file

    b. copying and pasting a list

    c. employ a third-party service.

List

■ ■ tutorials

How do you want to add contacts?

One by one, manually

| ○ Upload a file, use an external service, or paste rows |

Import contacts

Upload file   Connect service   Paste from file   Migrate list

You must finish the upload procedure after adding your list.

Uploading a file

For imports, uploading a file is the default option. This can be achieved by:

❖ uploading the file by dragging it into the field, or

❖ selecting the desired file by clicking "Choose file" after looking through your documents.

Note: You can upload files in the following formats: CSV, TXT, VCF, XLSX, and ODS. The largest file size is 50 MB. Additionally, XLS files up to 10 MB in size can be uploaded.

Copying and pasting a list

Choose "Paste from file." Please keep in mind that each line can only contain one email address. The emails must be separated from any custom fields you want to add with commas. Press Enter to make a new entry. Examples include:

peter@aol.com,Peter,male,32(Enter)jessica@ hotmail.com,Jessica,female,44(Enter)james@ gmail.com,James,male,20(Enter)

Consequently, this is considered a manual method of entering lists.

Note: *Semicolons or spaces may also be used to separate fields within a row.*

Service connection

If you want to import a list once, you can connect to a third-party service. An API key, host address, username, and other details are required to establish the connection. Depending on the account you're trying to connect to, certain details may apply. When prompted, fill out the form's required fields with the appropriate data.

Completing the upload

1. Choose whether you want to update already existing data or add new data.

a. Add and update: By selecting this, you can update (overwrite) the information for current contacts while also adding new contacts.

b. Only add now: Use this only to add new contacts; don't use it to change the information for current contacts.

c. Only update existing: Select this to make changes to contacts who already exist.

2. A consent confirmation box should be checked.

3. Click "Next." This directs you to the page where you can give custom fields their columns.

4. Set the data in the file as the value for the custom fields in your GetResponse account. By selecting the Skip columns denoted by a "?" box, you can also avoid assigning custom fields.

5. Press the "Import" button.

Segments

A specific group of contacts discovered using particular search criteria and saved with a distinctive name is referred to as a "segment." Instead of keeping a group of contacts in a separate list, segments let you define a group of contacts using a specific set of search criteria.

Because they are dynamic, you don't have to manually add new contacts to a segment. They are automatically added to the segment as soon as they satisfy the requirements.

How to make a segment

You must select search criteria before you can create a segment.

a. Go to Contacts > Search

b. Click "Advanced Search" and start adding conditions or condition groups.

c. When finished, select "Save as segment." It will display a pop-up modal.

d. After giving the filter a name, press the "Save" button.

Click "Segments" at the top of the search page if you want to view or edit your segments. You can edit, copy, or remove custom filters by clicking the "Action" icon. Segments have a lot of applications. Some examples of what you can do with the segments you've made are provided in the list below.

❖ Maintain your contact list. To locate your segments, go to Contacts >> Segments. View or edit the contact information for any contacts that are included in your segments. Additionally, you can export contact details if you'd like.

❖ Send newsletters to a specific audience. For instance, you can send customized messages based on, among other things, customer actions, custom fields, tags, scores, and client requirements and preferences.

❖ Exclude certain demographics from receiving your messages. For instance, you are aware that certain lists' members prefer to receive messages with different content (less text, more video, or vice versa) or the same content delivered at various intervals. For these email addresses, you are free to create however many segments you require. You can choose not to include these recipients when creating a newsletter for these segments. By doing so, you can send them various messages within the same list and customize your communication to suit their needs and preferences.

Chapter 16

Forms

In the chapter "Form Page and Landing Page," I described what forms are. Forms can be in a variety of formats, depending on how you want to present them to your subscribers. The procedures listed below describe how to obtain the HTML opt-in code from GetResponse and add it to your WordPress website. Your WordPress website will be configured with this code.

❖ Click "Forms and Surveys" from the list of menu options in your GetResponse account.

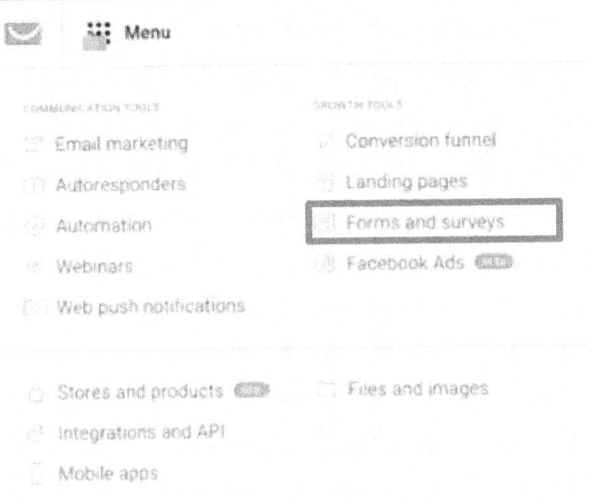

❖ You will be directed to a new page; scroll down and click the "Create Form" button.

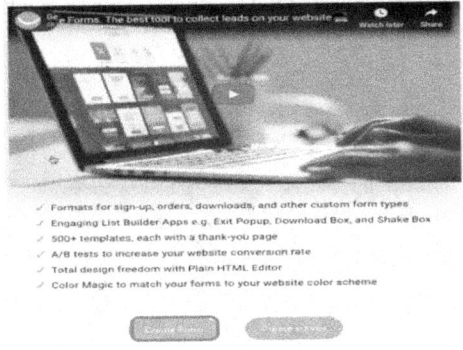

❖ You will copy the code and paste it on your website by selecting the "List Builder Wizard" option.

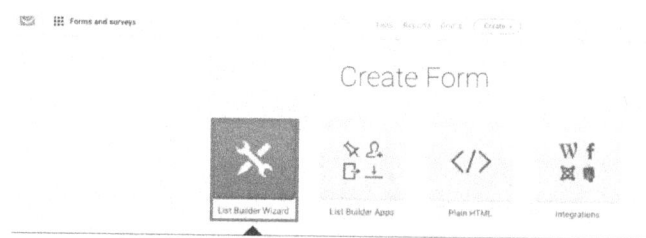

❖ You'll be taken to your form page after selecting a template. Drag and drop any form-builder fields provided to you on the page, such as an address, phone, company, fax, URL, etc., but the email address is a required field.

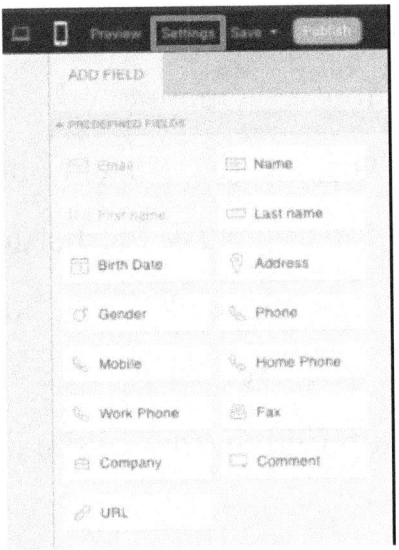

You'll find the word "Settings" at the top of the page; click on it. This will direct you to the next action.

❖ It is necessary to set up the "inputs and thank you page URL." You have the option to direct all sign-ups to a specific thank you page within the

GetResponse Form Settings. As was previously mentioned, make sure you've already created the form, and you must specify the list to which you want your subscribers to be added. After that, click the "Save" button in the top right corner of the page.

Click the "Publish" button on your form builder page.

❖ Install the HTML code on your WordPress website after copying it, and meanwhile, there will be three options provided for you to choose from.

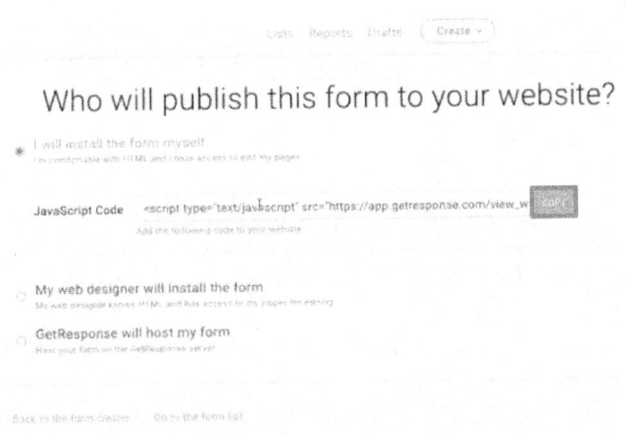

Chapter 17

Landing Page

You can use landing pages as one of your GetResponse account's list-building options. They enable you to entice customers to look at your offerings and subscribe to your list. You can either create your template from scratch or use one that has been expertly designed.

Before creating a landing page, you must first create a list. The goal of this is to turn your visitors into leads, and they can automatically become subscribers in the list you link to your landing page once they have entered their information, such as an email address, phone number, first and last name, etc.

To begin:

❖ Select "Landing pages" from the list of options in the menu of your GetResponse account. Select "Landing pages" from the list of options in the menu of your GetResponse account.

❖ Click the "create landing page" button.

❖ Choose a template from GetResponse's collection of expertly crafted templates. These templates are offered based on categories.

❖ Enter a name and click the "Use template" button in a pop-up modal after choosing the template you want to use. The template editor will then be displayed.

Customizing the template.

When it comes to creating and editing landing pages, GetResponse is regarded as the best among other email service providers. To create a captivating, mobile-friendly landing page for your company, simply follow the steps listed below:

❖ Double-click the text section you want to edit, then type in your own words. The editing tool menu becomes accessible. Use them to alter the text's style, arrangement, and positioning.

❖ Double-click the sign-up form to open the extra editing options, then make the following changes:

➢ To alter the text and formatting, click the form fields.

➢ Double-click the form to begin adding extra fields, such as consent fields and custom fields. You can collect contact information by using custom fields. When a contact signs up, consent fields give them the option to agree to your marketing or data processing policies. Click the "Webform fields" button to add the fields. Then, select the custom fields you want to use by clicking the "Custom fields" tab. To view the Consent Fields you've created in your account, click the "Consent Fields" tab. Then, pick the fields you want to include in the form.

❖ To further alter the appearance of your template, use the tools in the side toolbar. More sections, buttons, forms, shapes, videos, social sharing icons, and Paypal buttons can all be added.

❖ To A/B test your page design, include additional page variants.

❖ To create a mobile-friendly version of your landing page and make any necessary modifications, click the phone icon.

❖ Click "Next step" once you're satisfied with your design.

It must be made clear that lists must be created before landing pages can be created, or that if a list is already available, you can set up your landing page. The following plugins should be added to your Chrome Extension when using GetResponse to build a landing page that is appealing, responsive, and high-converting:

a. Color Picker Chrome Extension
b. Color Zilla (Advanced Color Picker)
c. WhatFont; this will create an exact color code for fonts and their sizes.

Changing the landing page's settings

❖ You can change the page title and add a description in the SEO settings. Your page will appear more prominently in

Google search results if you add a description. Alternatively, you can check the box to prevent Google from indexing your page (optional).

My landing page settings

SEO settings -

Page title

test1

This name will appear as the title of your page.

Description ⁱ

Don't index in search engines ⁱ

❖ Select the URL for your landing page in the landing page URL settings. Your landing pages are automatically published at one of GetResponse's subdomains. Additionally, you have the option of publishing it on your website or in a directory.

Landing Page URL settings ▲

Use one of GetResponse subdomains

https:// | test1 | gr8.com | ▾

Assign your own domain

GetResponse subdomains

+ Add a new domain

There are two ways to assign your domain to your Landing Page: Change DNS settings or Add a CNAME entry to your subdomain.

Note: *Lowercase English alphabet characters (a-), numeric values (0–9), and hyphens ("-") are acceptable in the landing page's URL. You cannot use diacritical marks, underscores, or other special characters.*

❖ Choose the "list" where your subscriber will be added when they sign up in the subscription settings. If the "confirmed opt-in" option is toggled on, double opt-in is considered to be enabled. Additionally, decide if you want to include a contact in an autoresponder cycle and set the thank-you page. If your company has a personalized page, you can select the "custom thank-you page" from the dropdown menu and enter the URL you want to direct visitors from your landing page.

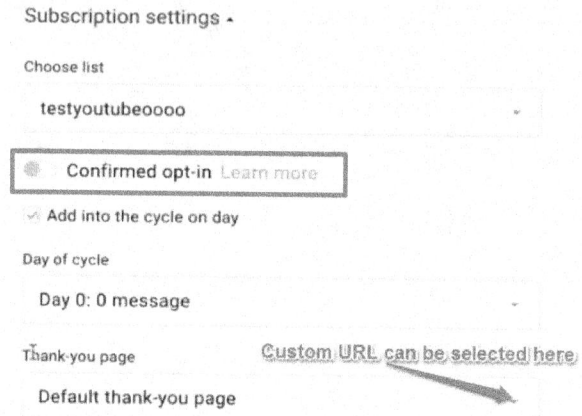

❖ Include a tracking code on your landing page for Google Analytics and Google Adwords.

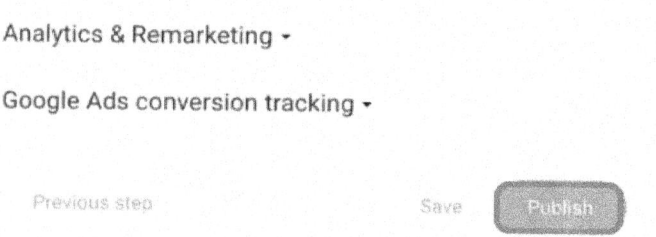

Click the "Publish" button when you have finished configuring your landing page. Once your landing page has been published, you can always obtain a link to it. To see how the link will appear to visitors to your landing page, copy it and paste it into the Google search bar.

Changing the DNS settings

If you want your domain name to be displayed in the landing page URL, you must update your nameservers (configure DNS) to point your domain to the GetResponse DNS server. For a domain that has nameservers set up, GetResponse allows you to create several subdomains. There is no need for another configuration.

Note: *Any email accounts you have on that domain will be disabled if the DNS for your domain is changed. Create a subdomain for your landing page and a CNAME record for that subdomain if you want to continue using emails on the domain you want to link to your page rather than changing the DNS.*

If you already have a website at your root domain, using a subdomain as your landing page is also advised. To change the nameservers, you must:

a. Access your hosting control panel by logging in.

b. Find the DNS settings under the domain settings section.

c. As the main and primary nameservers for your domain, utilize the following name servers:

★ ns-a-1.getresponse.com

★ ns-a-2.getresponse.com

d. Save your changes.

The propagation of changes across the internet (i.e., the updating of nameservers and cache records) can take up to 24 hours. You will receive a notification letting you know that the GetResponse team is investigating the records if you attempt to use an unverified domain when creating a landing page. There is nothing you need to do. Give the process up to 24 hours to complete.

If, after 48 hours, they are unable to verify your domain, you will also be informed. You will see a notification stating that they were unable to verify the domain if you attempt to use one. This merely indicates that there are no DNS records for the domain you want to assign. You should double-check your DNS settings if you get a message like that.

Chapter 18

Email Campaign

An email campaign is a planned series of email marketing messages sent at regular intervals to intensify a compelling case for purchase, subscription, download, etc. Each message should build on the one before it, offering pertinent new information, media, and links without losing sight of the "call to action." Email campaigns require careful planning, but they frequently yield higher returns because they provide the variety of contacts needed to close sales.

Every stage of the customer's life can benefit from email marketing campaigns, including brand awareness, brand knowledge expansion, interest generation for offers, action and conversation generation, relationship building, and converting current customers into ardent brand advocates.

A newsletter, autoresponders, transactional messages, and social media platforms can all be used to frequently contact your audience, resulting in better outcomes and a successful business.

With GetResponse, you can develop a useful marketing list of potential customers, partners, and clients, as well as a receptive and lucrative clientele. It ensures that messages arrive in recipients' inboxes with a deliverability rate of 99.5%.

Manage sales and marketing campaigns.

❖ Make use of a drag-and-drop newsletter editor with premade templates. Alternatively, you can use the HTML editor to create your template.

❖ Utilize autoresponders to automatically follow up with customers, sending them updates, offers, and a variety of friendly messages.

❖ To increase sales and manage and grow online sales, use the conversation funnel. The GetResponse conversion funnel is a comprehensive tool that can assist you in marketing and selling products online, locating potential customers, compiling contact lists, retaining customers, and boosting sales.

❖ To create a process that reflects the experiences of your customers, create automation workflows. This adaptable tool enables you to reward customer engagement and send messages based on their actions.

❖ With A/B testing of newsletters and landing pages, you can evaluate your marketing strategies.

How to set up a GetResponse newsletter, autoresponders, and automation workflow will be covered.

Newsletter

The simplest way to communicate with your customers is through newsletters. For example, extend a warm welcome to new clients, let them know about upcoming sales, invite current clients to sign up for a loyalty program, or send them a coupon code.

To create your newsletter in GetResponse, you can use either the drag-and-drop Email Editor or the HTML Editor. You can work with email templates and eliminate any coding requirements with the drag-and-drop editor. If you're comfortable with HTML coding, an HTML editor is a good option. A newsletter can be created and sent to your list by following the instructions.

The procedures for creating and sending a newsletter

❖ Select "Email marketing" from the menu in your GetResponse account.

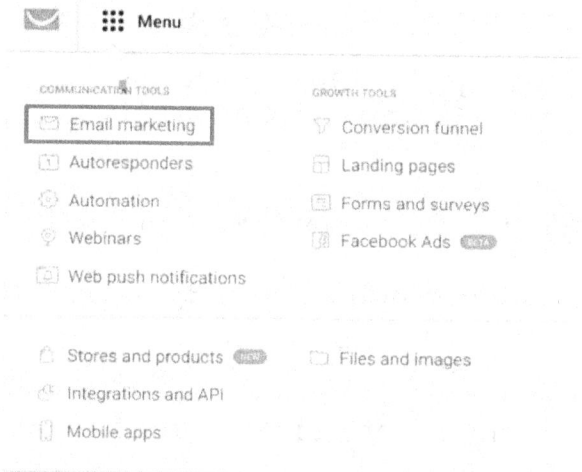

❖ Click the "Create newsletter" button under the Newsletter tab.

❖ Provide an internal name for your message.

❖ Choose "linked list" from the drop-down menu to send your newsletter to your audience.

Youtube Video Email Marketing

Edit name

26/100 characters. The name will appear on the list of your messages. Only you will see it.

Linked list

❖ Choose the "from" and "reply-to" addresses.

Note: *Your sending email address and the one used for replies from your contacts may be the same.*

❖ Give the subject for your message.

❖ Add recipients to the message by clicking the "Add recipients" button.

It is called a one-time email campaign or an email blast because the list you chose in step iv will be used in place of the recipients' addresses.

❖ Start designing your message by clicking the "Design message" button.

❖ Choose if you want to use "predesigned templates," "your templates," "blank templates," or design the message using an HTML editor.

❖ You will be taken to the message editor after selecting the template. The editor will open a window for HTML where you can enter your code. Your address and an unsubscribe button for your list to opt out are always displayed in the footer section of the message editor page.

❖ After finishing writing your message, click "Next" in the upper-right corner of the message page to proceed to the settings page.

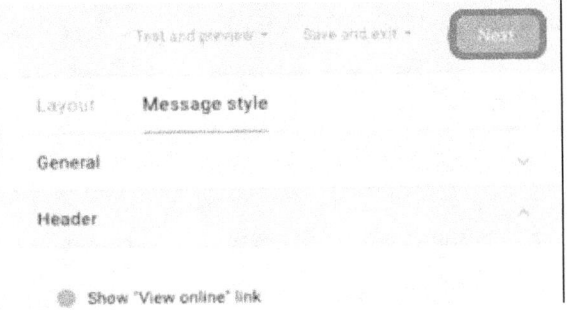

❖ Decide if you want to send the message to Google Analytics as a source.

❖ Determine whether you want to share the message's online version on Facebook or Twitter under the "Sharing" section.

❖ You have the option to either send the message "immediately" or "schedule it for later."

❖ Choose if you want to send it with perfect timing.

❖ Finally, you can choose to "Send message or schedule" or save the message as a draft. All of the contacts on the list you've chosen will receive your message, which will also be sent according to the schedule you've established.

Autoresponder

The term "autoresponder" refers to a series of follow-up messages. This means that to reach your chosen contact list, you will need to send out multiple newsletters. Thus, it is referred to as a "series of contents."

Steps for creating and sending an autoresponder

- ❖ Select "Autoresponders" from the menu in your GetResponse account.

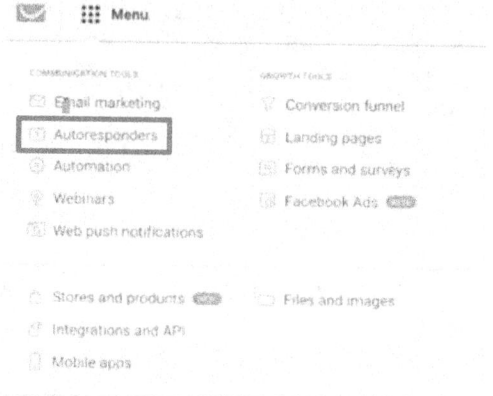

❖ Click the "Create Autoresponder" button to start writing your autoresponder message under the "Manage autoresponders" tab.

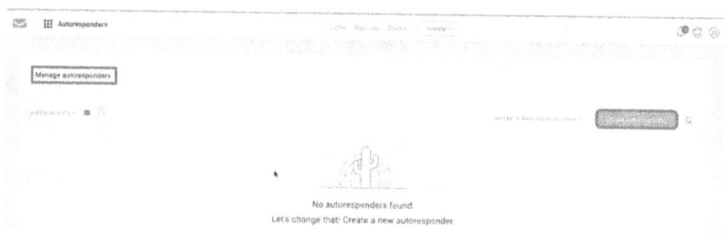

❖ Give your message an internal name.

❖ From the drop-down menu, select the list that is connected to the autoresponder. Your contacts will sign up for this list. Make sure to choose the same list for each autoresponder you plan to create if you want to create more than one in a cycle.

Welcome Email Series (New Blog Readers)

❖ Assign the autoresponder to a particular cycle day. For instance, messages begin on Day 0 (the contact's subscription day) and Day 1 (the contact's opt-in day). Depending on when you want an autoresponder message to be sent, you assign each new one to a particular day of the cycle.

Choose whether you want the message to be sent "exactly" at a specific time, "with a delay of," or "at the same time as the signup time." Additionally, select the days of the week you want the message to be sent.

❖ Choose the "from" and "reply-to" addresses.

❖ Add the subject of your message. Put your name or your company's name in the subject line. It increases the open rate.

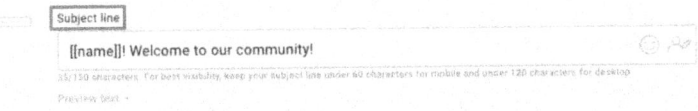

❖ Start designing your message by clicking the "Design message" button.

❖ Choose whether or not to send the message to Google Analytics as a source.

❖ If you want the message to go live immediately, click the "Save and Publish" button.

Finally, there is no restriction on the number of messages you can send from a single list. It's not advisable to send too many emails in a short period of time unless the recipient has specifically requested it. Otherwise, they might feel that you are sending them too many emails and decide to unsubscribe. You might also decide to add a new message, in which case you can do so by writing a fresh autoresponder message.

Every time you want to add more messages to your cycle to make it a continuous sequence, repeat the process.

Chapter 19

Email Automation

A marketing automation message is an exclusive message type used only as an action in marketing automation workflows. The main distinction between this message and others you can use with GetResponse is that you don't set the sending properties. The workflow's conditions and filtering are what cause the message to be sent.

The automation message management view will display a list of all recently created automation message drafts. It will contain both incomplete and workflow-ready messages, as well as those that are already in use and those that are currently in use. Both messages created using the previous message editor and the new one will be displayed in this view.

Anatomy of Email Automation

There are three questions you should consider and provide answers to before you begin creating email automation.

a. **Start**: Before you begin creating your automation, ask yourself, "How do I want to start?"

b. **Action**: You can customize your contact journey here. You'll ask yourself, "What do I want this automation to do?" Only you can customize the actions, settings, and features in the automation builder for each contact because there are so many available options.

c. **Stop**: You'll ask yourself again, "How do I want this automation to stop?" Getting an exit depends on your marketing strategies as well as on how you start and take action.

Note: *Having some tools ready is recommended. Consider how you'll interact with and respond to the actions of your subscribers.*

Steps for creating an automation message

How to create an automation message using GetResponse is described in the following steps:

❖ Select "Automation" from the menu of your GetResponse account.

❖ Click the "Create workflow" button located in the top-right corner of the page under the "Workflows" tab.

❖ A selection of templates will be presented to you, from which you can choose. Alternatively, you could start from scratch.

❖ As I did in the example, when creating email automation on the ActiveCampaign software, give your automation a name and select any block (element) as your starting point (trigger).

The "Chat24/7" button is located in the left corner of the automation workspace and can be used by beginners who are unsure of how to build automation using GetResponse.

The "Save and Publish" button is located in the top-right corner of the page. Click it once you're done creating your automation sequence.

Conclusion

Most of GetResponse's customers are small businesses with 1 to 50 employees who work in the marketing and advertising industry. It offers tools to help with enterprise marketing requirements as well as email marketing, auto-funnels, landing pages, and marketing automation. With the help of its essential email marketing features, users can send email campaigns, online surveys, newsletters, and follow-up autoresponders.

According to the customer's review, "GetResponse's visual campaign builder is excellent." It makes developing even extremely complex campaigns a breeze. It is among the best products currently available, in my opinion. It includes all of the features you would want in a sophisticated email platform. The foundation of GetResponse is this, and it excels at it.

Finally, GetResponse is intended to be an all-in-one online marketing tool that combines email marketing and online campaign management tools for overseeing sales, maximizing ROI, and using online marketing effectively.

www.ingramcontent.com/pod-product-compliance
Lightning Source LLC
Chambersburg PA
CBHW070526220526
45467CB00003B/867